Praise for

Surviving Sorrow, A Mother's Guide to Living with Loss, is gut-wrenching, honest, heartfelt, practical, and hope-filled. Kim's "Survival Steps" from her early days of grieving to years beyond provide insightful ideas to help any grieving mom (or friends, family members, pastors, or counselors who want to help a grieving mom) cope with hope. Her "Spiritual Steps" point grieving moms to biblical truth and the God of all comfort, who meets us where we are, and helps us step forward, in our healing, heavenward journey. I'm adding *Surviving Sorrow* to my "must have" resource companions, and encourage you to also!

KATHE WUNNENBERG | Bereaved mom, Founder/President of Hopelifters Unlimited, and author of *Grieving the Loss of a Loved One*

Powerful. Poignant. Personal. If you've lost a child and need to learn how to breathe again, this book is for you. With vulnerable openness, gut-level honesty, raw emotion, and rediscovered joy, Kim Erickson will guide you step-by-step to a place of renewed faith and emotional healing. *Surviving Sorrow* is filled with biblical wisdom and meaningful action steps. It's also an ideal gift for friends who experience this unthinkable loss.

CAROL KENT | Speaker and author, *When I Lay My Isaac Down*

We are stewards of all we've been given. In this book, Kim Erickson stewards deep pain and loss. Though it is a survival guide, the story brims with life and hope. May you experience that in your heart as you read.

CHRIS FABRY | Host of *Chris Fabry Live!* daily radio program

I have read more than a dozen books to help myself and others with grief through the years. I plan to use this one as a primary recommendation moving forward. Kim vulnerably and courageously revisits her own pain, her deepest, darkest brokenness to love you, truly help, and walk hand in hand with you so you will survive the darkest days and thorniest thoughts after loss of life. There are so many helpful insights, and practical touches of healing balm primarily for those who've lost a child! And even though I've not experienced this loss specifically, the deepest of griefs, each page lifted me on my journey, and will continue to strengthen my own sorrow survival.

CHUCK PETERMAN | Lead Minister, Creekside Christian Church, St. John's, FL

Kim does an amazing job of helping grieving parents walk through their journey of grief after the loss of a child. I wish this book was around when my husband and I were grieving the loss of our son after he died. I love how real and honest she is with the ebbs and flows of grief and how she offers tangible ways to heal and take steps forward to live despite the pain of our loss. Kim is living proof there is life after loss.

HEATHER GILLIS | Bereaved mom, www.heathergillis.com

There is something about the journey that, when someone has traveled it, gives different insights, a different level of compassion with the same truth. A depth and richness of understanding that has "been there," has grieved the incredible loss, has walked through the fire, and has ultimately found God's grace, peace, and hope. That is why I highly recommend Kim's book to you if you have or are walking through that valley of having lost a child. Kim has been there. It's where she met Jesus. This book is part of that redemptive story that came through their loss. I am so sorry for what you are walking through, but I truly believe you will be helped by this book.

STEVE ENGRAM | Senior Pastor, Desert Springs Community Church, Goodyear, AZ

I wish I had this book available early in my grief journey. As a mom who lost my twenty-year-old son suddenly, I appreciate the way Kim tells what worked for her while gently suggesting both practical and spiritual ideas which can help others in their grief journey. If you have experienced the death of a child of any age, get this book. If you know someone who has experienced the death of a child and are looking for ways to help them through their grief, give them a copy of this book. Or better yet, read this book yourself and use the suggestions it contains to minister to your friend.

KATHLEEN B. DUNCAN | Bereaved mom and author of *God's Healing in Grief*

This book I'm sure was not an easy one to write. Rehashing these kind of memories . . . it's a tough thing, but out of love for you she makes it known that you are not alone in this struggle. Page after page, it's as if you're walking this journey with a dear friend. She's been where most of you are at right now. Her story will encourage you not to quit and be assured that there is joy on the other side of this cross that you are bearing. Wait and watch Him work in your life as you walk through this book. It's a must have, to those who want to make it, those who want to live again, and you will.

GAIL COOPER | Bereaved mom, speaker, and writer at GailCooperSpeaker.com

Could not put this book down! It was like Kim was in my head when she wrote this book! It has so much practical guidance to get you through each day and can be applied to many different kinds of loss of a child. I lost my baby in the second trimester and while I did not have the same memories with my baby, I knew her. I highly recommend this book to all the mamas out there with broken hearts no matter when you lost your child.

AMBER REED | Bereaved mom

How can there possibly be words for a circumstance in which there are none? With a steady outstretched arm of experience, this book provides something to cling to when the ground beneath you has fallen away and you've become engulfed in a bottomless pit of grief. Kim offers a tender touch of compassion and a firm grip to navigate the toughest steps of anyone's life. Like that best friend who just "gets it," she sits with you and holds you, giving you exactly what you need to take the next breath and the courage to exhale when you feel like giving up. This book is a lifeline for anyone consumed by sorrow or someone else trying to help them make it through.

ERICA WIGGENHORN | Bible teacher and author of *Unexplainable Jesus: Rediscovering the God You Thought You Knew*

surviving
sorrow

A MOTHER'S GUIDE
TO LIVING WITH LOSS

———

KIM ERICKSON

MOODY PUBLISHERS
CHICAGO

Unless otherwise indicated, Scripture quotations are from the ESV® Bible (The Holy Bible, English Standard Version®), copyright © 2001 by Crossway, a publishing ministry of Good News Publishers. Used by permission. All rights reserved.

Scripture quotations marked NASB are taken from the New American Standard Bible, copyright © 1960, 1962, 1963, 1968, 1971, 1972, 1973, 1975, 1977, 1995 by The Lockman Foundation. Used by permission. (www.Lockman.org)

Edited by Elizabeth Cody Newenhuyse
Interior design: Ragont Design
Cover design: Lauren Smith
Cover photo of paint in water copyright © 2016 by Milles Studio / Stocksy (1151727). All rights reserved.
Author photo: Daisy Moffat Photography

Library of Congress Cataloging-in-Publication Data

Names: Erickson, Kim, 1970- author.
Title: Surviving sorrow : a mother's guide to living with loss / Kim Erickson.
Description: Chicago : Moody Publishers, 2020. | Includes bibliographical references. | Summary: "Practical advice from one grieving mom to other grieving moms When Kim's three-year-old son died, she found plenty of resources on grieving. She says what she really needed, though, "was someone who would give me advice for living, not just grieving . . . How do I get through the grocery store without crying? What do I do with my son's things? When will my mind stop replaying the emergency room scene?" Now, ten years later, she's written that book"-- Provided by publisher.
Identifiers: LCCN 2019040232 (print) | LCCN 2019040233 (ebook) | ISBN 9780802419170 (paperback) | ISBN 9780802497864 (ebook)
Subjects: LCSH: Children--Death--Religious aspects--Christianity. | Bereavement--Religious aspects--Christianity. | Grief--Religious aspects--Christianity. | Mothers--Religious life. | Erickson, Kim, 1970-
Classification: LCC BV4907 .E75 2020 (print) | LCC BV4907 (ebook) | DDC 248.8/66--dc23
LC record available at https://lccn.loc.gov/2019040232
LC ebook record available at https://lccn.loc.gov/2019040233

Originally delivered by fleets of horse-drawn wagons, the affordable paperbacks from D. L. Moody's publishing house resourced the church and served everyday people. Now, after more than 125 years of publishing and ministry, Moody Publishers' mission remains the same—even if our delivery systems have changed a bit.

Moody Publishers
820 N. La Salle Boulevard
Chicago, IL 60610

1 3 5 7 9 10 8 6 4 2

Printed in the United States of America

*To my mom, a strong woman who has walked this road
more than once with two sons and a grandson.
Her quiet strength inspires many.
I'm so thankful to have a mom like her.
Love you, Mom.*

*Also, since I've reminded others not to forget the dads
who've lost children, this book is also dedicated to my dad,
because he's lost two sons and a grandson as well.
I'm grateful for my family.
Love you, Dad.*

contents

dear mom in mourning:

I'm so sorry. There are no words. Nothing to say. No cliché, no pat on your back, is going to help you now. I wish that you weren't reading this book as much as I wish I didn't have to write it. Yet here we are. You and me, our children gone. Never to return. Oh, the gaping, open wound of being without our child is too much to bear. Our heart searches in vain for what other choices we have. Searching, searching for a way back in time. A way back to before. A way back to our child. But none can be found.

No help is coming. Nothing will ever be the same. Nothing will ever feel right again. Won't someone please help?

Oh friend, I remember all of these feelings. I remember the confusion. I remember feeling lost. I remember all the questions. Like being struck blind and deaf. Nothing made sense. Life was suddenly too complicated and so simple all at once.

People tried to be helpful, but they couldn't relate. No one would dare tell me what to do, how to get through this. They just couldn't imagine it. They didn't want to hurt me or add to my pain, so mostly they stayed silent while I needed answers about how to do life without my son.

My hope is to provide this lifeline to you during your time in the pit of grief. I've been there. I never want to go back. Yet I remember the way out. I remember the steps, one heavy foot after the other. So that you don't have to walk it alone, I'll go in there with you. Back to the pit where my son is gone and there's no hope for a happy life. Ever. Again.

Why? Why would I go back where there is more pain than a heart can comprehend?

I'll go back through my grief because it's where I met God. Through the mire, muck, and dark, throbbing grief, God showed me His face, His heart. I know you might not be able to imagine it right now, but God is so much more than our minds can comprehend that I am now willing to reopen the wound, pick at the scab, and bleed all over again IF it means that one more person can see God in that dark, heart-shattered place.

How could I let you stumble through these next years when I have some ideas to make it a bit easier?

How could I let you sit there all alone when I know the way out?

My hope is that this book is as practical as it is spiritual. Being a mom who has lost a child is so difficult. As a teacher, my soul longs to lead you and give you some hope and direction. There are no easy answers. No cheat sheets to let you sail through this test. This will be the most difficult thing you will ever do. Living while grieving will bring you to your knees, but you *can* do it. You *can* go on living. Little by little. Step by step. I promise you. I'm living proof.

I can almost hear you crying out now, "Not me. I am not going to be able to do this." Or, "I'm afraid. I don't know if I can." Deep in your soul, you know that your life will never be the same. It will never be okay. Losing your child is not something you will *ever* get over. I agree. No question.

I'm only here to help you see how life could move forward in a different way. I know you don't want this different way. You want your child back, your life back. But, friend, that's not going to happen. So what choice do you have but to try? Try to unfold yourself from the fetal position on the floor, pick yourself up, and keep putting one foot in front of the other. I'd like to give you some advice about how I—and others—have crawled down this ragged road of grief. I want to be here for you. To weep along with you. To lift you up a little on the rough spots. To show you the way out.

The goal of this book is to ease your path in the pit of grief, to give you some ideas to avoid painful detours, and to help you understand that you are never alone.

Please, take my hand. Borrow my hope. Allow me the privilege of walking beside you.

Sorrowfully,
Kim

how to use this book to help your healing

This book is meant to be a survival guide, a tool for moms. Like a travel guide or well-worn map, I hope you go right to the information you need most. Feel free to write in this book, dog-ear the pages, and throw it across the room when you need to do something to express your grief. It's okay. Go ahead and use this book like a shovel or a screwdriver: pick it up when you need it, put it away when you don't.

Please feel free to jump in and out of chapters when you encounter those topics. You don't need to read this book straight through. It's not a novel (we wish, right?!). Take your time. Read what applies to you, then set it aside for a while. Try some of the suggested ideas. Use what appeals to your heart and disregard the rest. I'm no expert. I'm just a mom, with a child gone from this earth for over a decade, who hopes to give you some practical help to get through the devastation of living without your child.

If you find this book helpful, would you please email me? As I'm sure you can understand, it would help me to know that losing Austin, living all these years without his sticky fingers and one-of-a-kind personality, has resulted in *something*—something good or helpful to others. It would help me to hear that all the tears and tough days that went into writing this book helped you in some tiny way. You can contact me through my website at KimAErickson.com. Thank you!

my story

It was April 2008. I was married to Devin Erickson, the man who stole my heart and made me laugh. We had two healthy, active little boys. Austin had just turned three, and Ethan was fifteen months. I had a great job. We lived in my dream house, pool and hot tub included. I thought our life was just about perfect. We were so happy.

Austin was diagnosed with strep throat on a Tuesday morning. The typical week with a sick kid rolled on. Medicine, taking turns with the boys, doctor visits. But we were worried. Something was off. Austin was normally a tornado, unstoppable. And he was down, floppy, breathing so heavily.

We took him back to the doctor three days in a row. The doctors told us, "Don't panic; it's just strep throat." Or, "Give the medicine time to work." So that's what we did.

We waited. We kept giving him the medicine. He stayed on the couch, asking for more medicine because his throat hurt so badly. On Thursday night, he woke me up at about 4 a.m., saying, "Mom, I wanna brush my teeth."

"Okay, angel. How's your throat?" I asked.

"It hurts. I wanna brush my teeth," Austin said again.

"Let's go," I said, and, looking at the time, "it's time for you to take more medicine anyway."

I set him up with his toothbrush and went downstairs to get his medicine. When he took the medicine, he groaned in pain. As I tucked him back into bed, I asked him to take some swallows of water from his sippy cup. He groaned again.

"You're a tough cookie," I said as I smoothed the wisps of his soft blond hair over his forehead.

"I'm a tough *cookie*?" he asked with his head tilted to the side, as if to say, "Silly Mom. Cookies are not tough!"

"Tough cookie means you are brave and strong," I replied, grinning. Austin was always asking questions upon questions. Always.

"I *am* a tough cookie!" he declared. And he curled up with his blanket.

"Love you," I said as I turned out the light.

"Love you," Austin murmured.

I stood there a moment, as I often did, looking at my son in his bed, wondering how I got so lucky to have this incredible kid. I went to check on the baby in the next room, and then I tried to go back to sleep. It didn't work. My job was incredibly stressful that week, and I was working on an important deadline that could not be moved just because my son was sick. I gave up on sleep and got ready for work. Before I walked out the door around 6 a.m., Austin and Ethan were still sleeping. I kissed their little heads and went to work, even as I longed to stay home.

At about 9 a.m., I received "the call." If you're reading this book, I don't need to say anything else. "The call" is the one every parent dreads. It's the one call you fear above all other things. The moment in time that you will remember, unfortunately, for the rest of your life.

The nanny was screaming, "Austin . . . ambulance . . . come home!" over and over again. I dropped the phone and ran out of my office. One of the assistants in our unit grabbed my keys from me and drove me toward home.

I didn't know what to do. My mind couldn't even really comprehend what was happening. All I could think of was that I wanted to be there, with Austin, right then. But the drive was at least twenty minutes long, even going eighty miles per hour down the freeway.

No, I didn't pray. I didn't think about God at all. God never came to mind in that moment. At that time in my life, God had no place at all. We didn't go to church; we didn't pray as a family. I didn't even teach my boys about God. God was nowhere to be found in our lives.

Oh, I think both Devin and I would have said we believed in God and had "faith," but beyond that, no part of our lives showed any relationship with God. So, when that call came, I could only think of Austin. In my heart and my mind, silently, I cried out to Austin: "Austin! Can you hear me? Austin! Do you hear Mommy? I need you to fight, Austin. I need you to stay here with Mommy. Can you hear me, Austin? Do you hear me? You fight! You keep fighting, Austin. I'm almost there, angel. Almost. Keep fighting. Stay here with Mommy, okay? You have to keep fighting. Please, Austin, stay with Mommy!"

That's when something happened to me. Everything stopped. I was no longer sitting in my car.

There were no noises. No highway. Nothing. Nothing but a sweet, clear voice in my heart:

"But Mom, it's so pretty here . . . " I felt Austin say into my heart.

He said this with such longing. He wanted to stay where he was. In that moment, I felt so wonderful. I cannot explain it with words. Now, I can only describe it as though the hand of God reached down from heaven and placed it over me.

I was completely overwhelmed with love, peace, and purity. I somehow knew that Austin was feeling what I was feeling. I thought about what he said, "But Mom, it's so pretty here." I also felt how much he wanted to stay there, wherever he was that felt so amazing. It was so wonderful that, as a mom, there was only one choice:

"Okay, angel," I responded in my heart. "Okay."

Then it was over. I was back in my car roaring down the highway. I looked over at my coworker driving the car. She didn't notice a thing. But I knew Austin was gone. I sat there in silence. Stunned at what just happened.

I thought about it. "But Mom, it's so pretty here." Longing to stay. Feeling wonderfully, unexplainably loved, with such purity and completeness.

"That was heaven," I thought. I had no doubt about it. Heaven was a place. An amazing place, beyond words, beyond our imagination. Heaven was a physical place, like a city we could travel to in a car or on an airplane. Heaven was real.

Austin was there. I was certain of it. Austin was safe in heaven. Not only safe, but he was feeling and experiencing perfect love.

Eventually we arrived at the hospital. I watched them try to revive Austin, pumping his heart, pressing his little chest so hard. I stood next to his head and smoothed his hair over and over again. I tried to "reach him" again, but nothing happened. I knew it wouldn't, but the mom instincts kicked in and all I wanted was my son back.

After about an hour, I asked them to stop. Just stop.

"Please, stop," I said. "It's okay. He's not here. He's gone."

"I want to try one more thing," the doctor said.

I agreed and then took another walk in that hospital hallway. It was difficult to watch them work on my little three-year-old. He looked so tiny in that hospital bed.

Devin hadn't arrived yet because the police were at our home. A child had been found unresponsive in our home, so the police had a job to do. I understood this, especially since I had worked the "abuse and neglect" unit as a prosecutor-intern during law school. I understood the procedures.

Finally, Devin arrived at the hospital. The love of my life looked like a different man already, bent and broken in grief. I believe the doctor was really waiting for Devin to arrive before he pronounced Austin dead. At last, the doctors and nurses stopped working on Austin.

They told us we could have up to two hours with him. We

sat with Austin until his body grew cold. After that, I couldn't bear any more. I simply could not touch him or sit beside him anymore. My mind couldn't take in what was happening.

Next, we were all interviewed by the police. Me, Devin, and the nanny, Miss Alma, each sat with investigators as they questioned us, separately, about Austin's strep throat, steps we took, medicines we gave. The works. When we were finally allowed to go home, police tape was wrapped around our front door. Everything seemed unreal, in slow motion.

The officers were leaving and took the tape down, apologizing and saying they were sorry for our loss. It would be the first of what seems like a million times we've heard "sorry for your loss" since that day.

Next came the autopsy, required by law since Austin had died in our home. The medical examiner told me she can usually determine a cause of death, but in Austin's case, she could not determine which system failed first. While strep infections can go to the heart or cause a person to go septic, neither of those things happened to Austin. In fact, he had no strep bacteria remaining in his system when everything was tested. Austin's throat, however, was nearly swollen shut. So, on his death certificate, it states that Austin died from complications with strep throat.

But that wasn't all.

Later, a pediatric expert reviewed the files and noted that many of Austin's major organs were somewhat swollen. He suggested that a test for mononucleosis be performed. It came back positive. So Austin actually had strep throat and mono.

Ultimately, the experts believe that Austin did not get enough air, and eventually his body began to shut down.

We learned about all of those medical issues much later. But first we had to get through the funeral. Somehow.

All the people, all the food. We requested "no flowers, please" because I cannot bear the sight or smell of "funeral flowers." We lost my brother Jeff back in 1989 in a car accident. I was nineteen and a freshman in college. Losing Jeff devastated our family and touched our small community. Funeral flowers flowed in the door in what seemed like every hour. There was no way I could do *that* again.

So, cards poured in. Phone calls never stopped. Question after question. Tissue after tissue. Almost all of it a blur now.

There are two things that are *not* a blur to me as I write this book. The first is that Friday-morning moment where I believe I felt a tiny bit of God or heaven around my soul as Austin passed from this earth while I was still in my car trying to get to him. The second crystal-clear moment took place just two days later, when I insisted on going to a church I had visited a couple of times. Let me back up for just a moment so I can explain how this happened.

A few months before Austin died, Devin and I agreed that we should probably start dragging our kids to church like our parents had with us. We wanted them to believe in God, to have "faith." So we agreed that I would "shop" for churches while Devin stayed home with the boys on Sundays. I tried several in the area, but landed on one I wanted Devin to try. In fact, the Sunday before Austin got sick, I had visited Desert

Springs Community Church in Goodyear, Arizona, for the second time. I came home that Sunday and told Devin that I thought I had found a church I could "tolerate" taking our boys to on Sunday mornings. I was so very far away from God at that time! Devin agreed that we would try that church the following Sunday as a family.

But Austin ran a fever the next day, on Monday. Tuesday he was diagnosed with strep throat. Friday he did not wake up from his bed. On Saturday, I called that church to inquire about holding Austin's funeral there, even though they didn't know us. On Sunday, I was so positive that I had encountered God in my car as Austin passed from this earth that I insisted we go to church that day, just like Devin said we would the week before. My family was shocked. I was the "black sheep," the one who never went to church. I was surprised myself, but something deep in my heart made me certain we *had* to go that morning.

I'll be forever grateful for that church and its people. At the end of the service, the pastor asked anyone who had never turned their life over to Jesus to consider doing that right then that morning. I knew that I had never committed myself to Christ, had never accepted that Jesus was the Savior of my soul. But that moment in the car was so powerful, I knew it was real. I had to push my doubts aside and go with my heart. As the pastor asked for everyone to bow their heads and close their eyes, I made my decision. I was going to give my life to Jesus right then and there. As the pastor prayed, so did I.

Next, the pastor had no idea we might be in church that

day, but he asked the church to join him in praying for a family that had just lost their three-year-old son and had no church home. It took me a moment to realize he was talking about us! Many of my family members, including me and my husband, nearly fell down sobbing as the entire church began to pray for us. Several of them must have realized it was our family because they came around us and laid their hands on us as they prayed. As we walked out, many of them were crying, too. It was the most beautiful experience.

So I remember that Sunday, April 27, 2008, just days after Austin died, in crystal-clear high-definition because I gave my life to the Lord that morning. I finally set aside my stubborn heart and accepted that Jesus Christ was my Savior and that my faith in Him would save me from my sins and restore my relationship with God.

We held Austin's memorial service at that church I had attended a grand total of three times. We had no idea what we were doing, but we just did what seemed right to us. We played music Austin loved while pictures of him flowed on the screens. His huge grin (usually covered in food) was a perfect reflection of the crazy kid he was in those three short years.

After the funeral, everyone began to leave. Devin and I began to try to live while drowning in the worst sorrow imaginable. As much as we sometimes wanted to give up, we had Ethan. Sweet, adorable, steady Ethan was only fifteen months old. He really didn't seem to have any idea that something horrible had just wrecked our lives.

Even today, it is difficult to know who was "clinging" tighter, us or the baby. Looking back, I have so many pictures of me or Devin holding Ethan in those first months after Austin died. Not to put any pressure on him, but that baby was (and perhaps still is) our lifeline. One picture in particular comes to my mind as I write: Ethan was about two years old and sound asleep on his daddy's chest. You might think "awww, so sweet" when you first see it. That is, until you see his daddy's eyes. The depth of sorrow on his face is palpable. That man loved Austin so much it nearly crushed him.

If you're reading this book, I'm fairly certain you feel like losing your child is going to crush you. It could. It might. Losing a child is a weight like no other. It's strange, though, because no matter how short the time on earth, most parents would take the exchange of that burden: have your child and lose him/her too early over never having the blessing of your child at all, never meeting him/her, never holding him/her. Even though you never knew you could experience such pain, on most days, you wouldn't give up minutes, let alone days or years with your child.

On other days, the dark pit of grief seems so endless and hopeless that thoughts *do* enter your mind that it might have been easier if your child had never been born. Or you might entertain thoughts that it would be easier if you went to sleep and never woke up again. The pain is simply too much.

These thoughts are not easy to admit, but I can promise you this: if we continue on this journey together, I will always tell the truth and I won't sugarcoat our pain.

So what do we do now? We are being crushed in the pit of grief. Everyday life seems insurmountable, heavy, unbearable. We are wearing cement shoes, carrying a heavy, wet blanket, and trying to navigate our way up a steep climb. We are exhausted, but this is where we begin to walk together.

How did I get through it? Only by the grace of God. How

do I continue to get through it? Only by the grace of God. A friend who came to Austin's memorial service gave us something that helped me every day during those first few months, and probably a thousand times since. It was a photograph of a rare flower and below the picture was this verse from the Bible:

The Lord is near to the brokenhearted
and saves the crushed in spirit.
(PSALM 34:18)

what I want you to know before we jump in

Since that final moment with Austin, and my tiny glimpse of what heaven feels like, I knew that heaven was real. As I read this verse, my mind thought, "I sure want to believe this is a true statement. I guess we're going to find out." But my heart cried out in a silent, but louder voice: "Oh God, let this be so! Please God, I am brokenhearted. Are You really there? I am totally crushed in spirit. I can't even seem to get enough air in my lungs. God, save me from this pain!"

I didn't know anything about my Bible yet, but each time I looked at that picture and cried out to God, a calm came over me. A deep breath often came next. It became a mantra of sorts. Whenever I felt like I simply couldn't take any more of this grief, I would repeat these words in my head. Sometimes, when grieving and the looming loss of Austin made me mad, I would almost shout the words and stomp my foot, demanding that God be near to me and save me from being crushed in the pit. Now!

Sometimes people are shocked that I would shout, stomp, or demand anything from God. Perhaps it doesn't sound very respectful or very "Christian-like." But it's the truth. The reason I feel okay about being "real" in my relationship with God is because the Bible says that when we accept Jesus as our Savior and Lord of our life, we become a child of God. As believers in Jesus, we are adopted into God's family. God becomes heavenly Father to us.

"Wow," I thought when I truly understood this new relationship I had with God. Just wow. Awestruck. The Creator of the universe is my Dad? As this settled over my heart, I thought of the type of parents Devin and I tried to be for Austin (who threw plenty of fits), and are trying to be for Ethan (who never throws fits). We love them unconditionally, regardless of any temper tantrums. We tell Ethan that he can tell us anything, that he can be honest with us about anything. We want him to tell us how he is feeling. As parents, we want our child to trust us with his deepest emotions and hurts. We want to know what's going on so that we can love him and help him through it if we can.

If I feel this way as a mom—human and struggling with all my own issues—then how much more must God desire the same thing from us as our heavenly Father? If God is really my Dad, then I should be able to go to Him with my real emotions. Please understand that while we want Ethan's trust and close relationship, we also still demand the respect a child should afford their parent. He's still the kid, and we're still in charge. It goes the same way with me and God.

Although I may "pitch a fit" sometimes and shout, stomp, and demand, I try not to cross the line into disrespect. The "demand" usually relates to a promise in the Bible—something God has promised to us as His children. The shouting and stomping is just the pain coming out. I believe God understands my pain. After all, God sent *His* only Son, Jesus, to earth where He would be disrespected, spit upon, whipped, and tortured to death on a cross. Oh how God's heart must have torn apart at the way His son was treated!

And, because Jesus was paying the price for our sin, God had to turn His mighty back on His own Son. Jesus had to take the pain of all our sin so that we could be forgiven and adopted back into God's family. If you can truly wrap your mind around what happened (and it's not easy), then you can grasp how God really does understand the pain of losing a child. He gave His only Son *for you*. God gave His only Son to die so that *you* could join the family of God and have eternal life in heaven. It's beyond our human comprehension. We'd never willingly give up our child for someone else. God, however, is not human, and He does not have our limitations. Plus, He knew the ending—His Son would rise again to be the Savior of the world and Ruler of the eternal kingdom.

> I began a lifelong journey of balancing my grief against my hope in heaven.

Of course, I didn't know any of this when I lost Austin. I didn't know God at all. I only knew *about* God, and I wasn't sure the story about Jesus was true. But in that moment when Austin died, I suddenly understood heaven was real. It wasn't until I began reading my Bible and meeting with other women (who knew their Bible inside and out) that I began to understand who God really is, who Jesus is, and what is yet to come. My Bible became my lifeline in the pit of my grief.

And . . . I still desperately wanted my son back. Even though I knew with every fiber of my being that Austin was with Jesus, oh, how I wanted him to be with us! I began a lifelong journey of balancing my grief against my hope in heaven.

While I discovered so many amazing things, the most important during my time of deep grief were two simple things. These two things I hold as absolutely true:

- Heaven is a real place.
- God does what He says (in the Scriptures) He's going to do.

After Austin died and I knew that heaven was real, and after I gave my life to the Lord on that Sunday morning, I started to search for what else was true about God. I had been ignoring Him my entire life, but now I wanted to know everything. My lawyer mind sifted through my questions and my Bible in order to determine if there was any evidence to support what I experienced that morning when Austin died.

I found the evidence. Over and over again. I learned by reading my Bible that God keeps His promises. From the very beginning, He promised that a Savior would come and rescue mankind from the sin that separated us from Him. God did it: He sent Jesus. Jesus promised He was preparing the way for us, that we would join Him in heaven. Jesus did it.

While these are the most important promises I found in my Bible, these are backed up by hundreds more. Even though I didn't understand how a loving God, a Daddy-God, could allow us to lose Austin, I did grow to trust Him. I feel as though I got to know God through my Bible and my "talking" with Him. As I learned more about God, the sharp edges of my grief began to get smoothed over. The crushing and never-ending burden of missing my little tornado became a bit lighter and easier to walk with through life. I learned to give some of my deepest pain to my Father God. I began to trust that He loved me, despite the pain He allowed in this life. I began to allow Him to lift the pain from my heart.

God Is Waiting . . .

He will do the same for you. Why am I so sure? Because God does what He says He's going to do. Period. End of discussion.

Jesus came to save every single person on earth, including you.

Even if you've rejected, mocked, or ignored Him your whole life like I did, God is waiting, patiently and forevermore, to have His daughter back. All you have to do is take one step into His arms. He's not far away, even if it feels that way in the middle of your grief. It's only because losing a child can block everything else in life out. I promise you that things will be different if you take that one step toward Him.

If you've never accepted Jesus as your Lord and Savior, you can do that right now by praying (and meaning in your heart) this prayer:

God, I don't know where to begin. I don't know anything right now. I hurt so much. But, I do believe that Jesus was Your Son and that He came to save me from my sins. God, I do know that I am a sinner who needs a Savior so that I can know You and have eternal life with You in heaven. I want to turn away from anything that is not pleasing to You. I want Jesus to be my Lord and Savior so that all my sins will be forgiven. Thank You, God, for loving me enough to send Jesus to save me. Jesus, thank You for being my Lord and Savior and granting eternal life to me in heaven. Amen!

If you prayed that prayer for the first time, welcome into the family of God! You are now a daughter of the King, a daughter of God. You are on a new journey through this life.

What If You're Not Sure?

Now, if you didn't feel anything, please don't worry or let your skepticism win. Accepting Jesus as your Lord is the best thing you can do right now, but it's not an immediate cure for the pain or troubles in your life. Today was just the first step.

A very important and life-changing step, but not a "minute clinic" cure. Getting to know the God of the universe is a life-long journey.

If you *didn't* pray the above prayer, and you aren't sure about Jesus and your faith journey, that's fine too. I truly understand how it feels to be unsure or skeptical. I remained in that same mindset for many years before Austin died. I also know that, right now, you have a lot to deal with in your heart and your mind to survive this loss. My hope is that you would not allow anything to stand in the way of this book helping you. There is a lot of practical advice in this book designed to guide you through living with loss. My heart is to hold your hand through this journey, not to judge you or push you about God or Jesus. Just use the parts of this book that are helpful to you.

If you already began your journey of eternal life because you became a daughter of God long ago, you know that the road is complex and challenging. Right now, you might be feeling like God forgot about you or betrayed you. Or, you might be mad enough at God to want out of this family, for good! I get it. I am often "sad-mad" and have a tough time interacting with God. When this happens to me, I need to take a walk outside. As nature reveals its complexities and beauty, I remember that God, who created all of these wonderful things, must know something I don't know. God must be doing something that I cannot possibly comprehend.

When the "why did this have to happen, God?!" days consume me, I remember those hundreds of promises that God made and kept as described in my Bible. I remember that God does what He says He's going to do, which means that *someday* He is going to fix this.

Someday, God will take me to Heaven. Someday, there will be no more mourning. Someday, there will be no more death. Someday, God will make a new place where I will be with ALL my kids and there will be no sadness or tears. Someday, there will only be love and joy, forever and ever. Someday.

Then, I blow my nose, splash some cold water over my swollen eyes, and wait for someday.

Someday gets me through the toughest days. The promise of "someday" can get you through your most difficult days, too. If you keep stepping into God and not away from Him, He will lift you, little by little, out of the pit of grief.

Someday.

Let's get started . . .

devastating details

The days, weeks, and months following a death are filled with tasks that simply must be completed and questions that must be answered. In those first few days, when you are still in the fog of disbelief, the details are devastating. The questions are never-ending, and the only person who can answer them is you:

What should be done with his body?

When and where should we hold the funeral?

What clothes will he wear as he lies in that coffin?

What type of casket will you choose?

What food?

What songs?

What pictures?

Where do you want the flowers?

When should I come? Where should I stay?

What will you wear to the funeral?

And on and on and on these questions come. Like waves of the ocean, knocking you down and keeping your head underwater. Yet someone must decide and tell people what to do.

I remember looking around at all the people in my house and wondering what I was supposed to do. It ended up feeling like a family gathering. Food arrived, coolers were filled with drinks, card games began, music was played.

And then someone would ask: "Do you want to choose some photos to be displayed at the service?"

"No, I'd rather die," my mind cried out, but silently. "Sure, let's do it," I responded.

What else can you do? There's no other choice. At some point, I felt if I heard, "Kim, do you . . . ?" one more time I might explode. Violence might ensue. Someone was going to get hurt. I couldn't take one more question from anyone.

The phone wouldn't stop ringing. People wouldn't stop talking. I needed some space. A whole lot of it. But that wasn't going to happen. Those next steps of handling the autopsy, cremation, and memorial service for Austin would not go away. There was no other choice but to keep putting one foot in front of the other, answering one question at a time. All the while feeling like I was drowning.

After that first week, there were still details to tend to and things that needed attention. People were mostly gone from our house, and it did feel less overwhelming. The house was growing quiet. Too quiet. Where was my little three-year-old tornado? Where were the shouts and hoots of laughter? When would I hear his running feet upstairs?

The devastating details of "Life Without Austin" now became what I dreaded. No noises of trucks or "diggers" hard at work on some imaginary building project. No shouts of "Mom, I need help with Ethan!" followed by a thud (pushing his baby brother away from his building, of course). No giggles or snuggles or the thousands of other things that make your house come alive as children live and grow.

I wished for the people to fill the house again so that I didn't have time to listen or think, only time to tend to all of them and answer questions. But I didn't really want all those folks back—I just wanted anything to occupy my mind. Anything but the reality of life without Austin. Anything at all.

> I needed something to do. Otherwise, I felt the details of daily life would kill me by thousands of tiny cuts.

Hello? Why is everything so quiet? What's that noise, deep inside me . . . soul groaning, spirit longing, heart weeping? How do I make *that* stop?

I ate a lot during those times. I cleaned the house, ran errands, read books. I needed something to do. Otherwise, I felt the details of daily life would kill me by thousands of tiny cuts. I would just bleed drops of grief each day, over and over again.

Making Decisions When You Can Hardly Think

After a few months, more things began to crop up for us to handle relating to Austin's death. We needed to get his death certificate. His remains needed to be buried. We decided to shelve that decision—literally—for the time being. We needed to obtain all of his medical records because the medical examiner encouraged us to hire a lawyer to look into Austin's treatment (what?!). How do we deal with that? Austin's college fund had to be transferred to Ethan or turned into something else. Who cares?

The waves kept coming and coming. Just when we thought our feet *might* be settling back under us, another piece of mail would arrive or a telephone would ring, and remind us that Austin was, indeed, still gone. Decisions we never dreamed we would have to discuss came like nightmares, suddenly and without warning.

Oh, did you think that you were climbing out of that slimy, dank pit of grief? "Think again," taunted the mundane things of adult life.

How can a mother's heart survive something that won't go away? Why do I have to keep feeling that stab to my heart? Isn't it enough already that Austin isn't here anymore?

Please know that those letters, phone calls, decisions, details, and tasks relating to Austin's death did eventually grind to a halt. At some point, all things are handled and taken care of. Just don't be surprised if it seems to drag on forever. Don't be alarmed if you feel like the number of matters you must tend to seems unfair and inappropriate, especially in those first few months.

If you are being buried alive by the devastating details of losing your child, please hold on a while longer. Just a bit longer, and you'll be able to breathe again. The tasks and technicalities of dealing with death will not completely overtake you. Those *will* subside. You can make it through this time period. Just take one day at a time.

To help with all of the details, we created a few different folders and boxes. A folder was made to sit right next to where we kept bills and important papers. Anything that needed action or a decision from us, we put the information in that folder. Telephone numbers, post-it note reminders, messages about the service, etc., went into that folder.

As gifts, plants, and cards arrived, someone was thoughtful enough to create a log for thank-you cards (sorry to say that never happened; I hope people understood). After some time, we created a box where things around the house that were distinctly Austin's could go to be put away for a while so our hearts could heal. Eventually, we made different boxes for his things: Austin—Keep, Hold for Ethan, and Give Away.

Don't ask me how we decided what went into each box! I have no recollection. I guess that's one of the marks of devastating details is that you are so overwhelmed by your grief that you don't remember much of it. When you look back, it feels like you were just on autopilot. Things just happened, but you don't remember exactly what steps you took or why you decided certain things.

In those early days, for survival's sake, I remember empowering others to take the lead in certain areas. I recall telling the women that they did not need to ask me about anything dealing with the house or meals. Unless it had to do with Austin or baby Ethan, they could do whatever they thought best. I didn't care what they decided to do with the leftover food or whether the sheets needed to be washed.

"Please," I said, "just handle it. Just do whatever you think is best. I promise we don't care. Whatever you decide will be fine."

You'll have to take them by the arm, look them straight in the eye, and give them permission. They won't dare make a move without your involvement or approval because the last thing your loved ones want to do is add to your pain or cause any difficulty.

Recently my brother Mark passed away from brain cancer. I decided to stay the week near his wife and four kids. I found myself asking his wife a thousand questions a day. I did not want to move Mark's water glass into the dishwasher if she wanted it to sit on the counter. Moving anything in the house that might remind her of Mark seemed too important for me to decide. Then one day, she cracked.

"Kim, I don't care! I cannot answer one more question. Everyone's asking me questions. I cannot deal with it," she sobbed.

I nodded and walked away, stunned that I had forgotten that time about ten years ago when Austin died and the questions nearly drowned me. How could *I* have forgotten?

Of all the people who should know how to behave around someone dealing with death, it should be me! Ugh. I felt like dirt. Stupid. Self-centered. Next, I felt grateful for her honesty. Without her telling me what she felt in that moment, I would never have had the flashback I needed.

That day made me look back on the memories I had of the people who had the guts to hang around my house after Austin died, and I saw them in a new light. I was even more grateful for them, more compassionate toward the questions. Questions were asked out of care for my feelings, not out of a lack of thinking before speaking.

If you are still in that season of constant questions, may I encourage you to consider that the people asking all those dreadful questions are doing their best to stand beside you right now. Be grateful for their courageous friendship. Go ahead and tell them you can't handle all the questions. Don't stuff it down inside like I did. Let it out like my sister-in-law.

It will take honest communication from you to help others feel empowered to step into your household or workplace. Consider putting one person, or a two-person team, in charge of certain things. One person to handle the flowers and cards. Two or three to handle the food and meals. Someone to organize and clean up. Divide and conquer! One of my dearest friends even took over putting together my outfit for the funeral service. She shopped, and I looked put together. I was so grateful!

I hope some of these ideas have helped you feel normal in the midst of all the craziness of this grief. It's normal to feel completely overwhelmed. Normal to be exhausted by everything and everyone. You are not alone. You are not weak or different from others who experience loss. What you feel is not exaggerated or overly emotional.

What you are feeling is to be expected (but no one talks about it). What you are feeling is part of the process of working through the loss (but no one warns you). Please be encouraged to take charge of the devastating details in a way that works *for you*. Below are some ideas to help you get started.

SURVIVAL STEP:
Delegate

So many people say, "Call me if you need anything." Yet how many people have you called to ask for help? My guess is none. I didn't either. We usually aren't very good at asking for help. When grief feels like it's swallowing you up, when you don't even know what you might need help with, asking for help seems like it's too much to figure out. It sounded like this in my head: "What *do* I need help with? Who would I ask? No one can help me anyway. No one can fix my problem. There's no one who would want to be around me right now. Oh, never mind!"

After all these years have gone by, I've come to believe that people really do want to help you; they just don't know *how or what* to do. So you are going to have to spell it out.

Ideas:

- Make a list (or lists) of what needs to be done. Include everything you can think of, not just tasks dealing with your loss, but literally everything rattling around in your (feeble due to loss) brain right now.
- "Chunk" the list above by using colors or drawing lines connecting items into categories such as: groceries, cooking, cleaning, funeral service, cards, memories, photos, post office, hotel rooms for service, shuttles to airport, work emails, etc.
- Have someone help you with the list, "chunking," and delegating.
- Choose friends or family members to take charge of each chunk, and then empower them to get these tasks completed, leaving you with only the items you alone must do.
- Tell someone you feel overwhelmed and that you need help.
- Ask someone to change your message on your phone to indicate you appreciate the call but may not return it for some time.
- Ask someone to set your email to indicate that you are away for a while and give another email or phone number if they need assistance right away.
- Turn off the notifications on your social media alerts (the less "noise" the better right now).

- Ask someone to pick up some folders or bins or boxes to help you get organized.
- Put a "we need" list on the fridge so that everyone can add to it (avoiding multiple trips to the store), and ask someone to make that trip to the store for you.

SPIRITUAL STEP:
Grab Some Time Alone

I know you feel so alone right now. Having a child missing from this earth feels like half your very person has been torn from you and hidden in a dark place where you'll never find it. The emptiness is terrifying. That feeling, however, is not true. It feels true, but it's not. There is a God, and heaven is real. There is hope.

Find a quiet place where you can be alone. Cry out to God. Yell at Him if you need to push aside your anger at this unfathomable situation. Try going outside, where God's creation won't be denied. The sunshine, air, birds, flowers will all declare the glory of God. The wind and sun on my face felt like the microwave "defrost" cycle for my frozen heart. Somehow the birds sang healing into my soul. A wilting flower reminded me that this world is temporary. Everything is dying.

You might think seeing everything dying would hurt me after Austin's death, but it revived me instead. The fact that the whole earth is perishing, that all things die and new things are born, was a reminder that heaven awaits. Eternal life is coming. *This* life, *this* earth is short and temporary. It also made me feel less alone. Grieving a child is a lonely road. It helped me to remember that all people, all things, experience death on this earth. I am not alone. Thousands upon thousands have lost children and have continued on with life on earth. Somehow, I would survive this pain.

You may find that people do not want you to be alone right now. They fear for your well-being. If you also fear being alone right now, that's okay. Just take one person with you who can be silent, who won't try to "help" you for those thirty minutes. Ask someone to walk silently with you.

If getting some time alone sounds too good to be true, you need to be assertive and make it happen. Tell someone you need to take a walk—alone. Tell them you'll only be gone thirty minutes and then you will be going into your bedroom for a nap. Even if you don't nap, thirty more minutes of quiet will do you wonders. You might find that people around you breathe a sigh of relief that you are taking care of yourself.

> You need to find a way to deal with the torture of living without your child.

Remember, even Jesus broke away from people, away from the apostles, to be alone. He would leave His closest friends and grab some space and time to be alone. Usually, He would pray. In my human mind, I also think He might have just closed His eyes and breathed deeply for a few minutes, perhaps gazing around at His beautiful creation. Jesus knew that He would be facing torture and death, so He made time to be alone with God.

I know what you're thinking right now: "I'll take it!"

I know that your own death, even if it involved serious torture, would be a relief from losing your child. I know you'd exchange places with your child. Since that is not our reality, you need to find a way to deal with the torture of living without your child. The point remains the same—when facing physical and emotional torment, Jesus took time to sit and pray in a garden, and you should, too!

Ideas:

- Take a thirty-minute walk, followed by a thirty-minute quiet time. If you nap after your walk, even better.
- Find a quiet place to sit outside; ask someone to make sure no one interrupts you.
- Take a drive to a park, pond, or nature preserve; get out and walk for a bit.
- Put headphones on (so no one talks to you), but don't listen to anything; let the silence and your own breathing bring calm to your inner self.
- Go ahead—lock your bedroom door for an hour!
- Take a journal or empty notebook, and write or doodle whatever comes to mind.
- Ask someone to pick up an adult coloring book and colored pencils; spend an hour in silence while you color.

- If anyone joins you, try for silence because your soul is bombarded with information it can hardly process right now. Give your heart a break.
- Do a craft that you used to enjoy (I know you can't imagine enjoying anything, but just do it to allow your mind something normal).
- Read a book if that usually relaxes you.

welcome to the crazy club

If you could just make it stop, you might be able to bear this loss. But it won't stop. The images in your head. The memories of each little detail surrounding the loss of your child. The thousands of things you should have done differently. The reasons why this is somehow your fault. The picture of his smile as he walked out the door. Her laugh as she pulled out of the driveway. His pain during yet another procedure. Her sweet smell the last time you held her.

Please, someone, stop the film! Can anyone help me stop seeing these images and scenes in my head? I can't stop them from being replayed over and over and over . . .

But wait! I couldn't bear it if these scenes were gone. Can someone help me make sure I don't forget anything about my child? Please, tell me I won't forget what his voice sounds like!

'Round and 'round the mulberry bush we go. 'Round and

'round on the carousel. Wanting to get off, needing to get off, but terrified we may never be able to find and hold those memories again.

Your mind feels so fragile. Most of the time, you feel like you're losing your mind. Losing those memories is a real threat. Losing a single memory feels like a life-or-death situation.

Welcome to the crazy club. If you feel like you don't have a firm grip on reality, or like your reality is simply full of scenes related to the loss of your child, then you're in the right place. You are a parent who has lost a child. Your mind now has a crack in it. Better to face it now than to ignore it.

It's also better to ask for help than to ignore it. There's no shame in asking for help. You need someone to talk to about the craziness in your mind. For me, it had to be an outsider. For some reason, I couldn't bring my grief to anyone close to me. I couldn't talk to anyone in my life about it. It seemed like talking about it might just be the hole in the dam that brought the whole ocean crashing through, and I wouldn't survive it.

Many people made suggestions about grief groups to join for support and understanding for our loss. Compassionate Friends and Grief Share were two common suggestions. For me, the idea of joining a group did not feel comforting. I did some research on these groups on the internet and gathered some information on what each offered. For some reason, however, the idea of sitting in a group of people in such pain felt like a heavy rock on my chest whenever I considered it. I figured that I just wasn't ready for that kind of thing.

In fact, my "solo" grief journey is one of the reasons I felt compelled to write this book. Not everyone is comfortable bringing their pain in front of others. If you're like me and you're not really open to sharing your grief with others, then my prayers have been answered because you have this book in your hands!

"It's called grieving"

All that being said, I really did need help. I finally saw a counselor about six months after Austin died. I knew my friend saw a counselor who was helping her a lot. I gathered the courage to admit I wasn't getting "better" and asked my friend for her counselor's name and number. I made the appointment, explaining that I was having trouble focusing and remembering things, especially at work. I didn't mention Austin because I thought I was doing fine in that area. But I couldn't read and comprehend most days. As a lawyer, that's your whole job, to read and comprehend, to write and explain. I couldn't do it. I would read and reread. I couldn't type a word. I kept going to the breakroom for . . . something . . . I just couldn't remember what. I'd leave the breakroom and trudge back to my office— only to find a bowl of soup for lunch, but no spoon. Spoon! That's what I went to the breakroom for, silly me. Back to the breakroom I'd go, only to forget yet again . . .

It was ridiculous. I had no idea what was wrong with me. I only told one friend about this particular crazy. She gave me the number of her counselor. I made the appointment after hanging up about twelve times. I didn't need a counselor after all. I was doing fine. I hated the thought of looking weak, pathetic. I hated the pity I could see on people's faces. I was fine. Leave me alone.

Finally, I decided to go. I was wearing a path from my office to the breakroom! When the counselor asked why I made the appointment, I described how I wasn't functioning at work, how I was forgetting everything. The minute something went into my brain, it was gone. I told her that my brain felt like a colander in my kitchen. I could pour something into it, but it would immediately drain out. No matter what I tried, I couldn't plug all those holes!

She asked what was going on in my life, whether I had any added stress lately. Initially, I answered, no. My job was the same. Same bosses, same office, same work. Always stressful, but that was normal. Somewhere in the middle of describing my life to her, I mentioned, "Oh yeah, we did lose our three-year-old son to strep throat about six months ago, but I'm doing okay with that . . . "

WAIT! "Did you just say that you lost your three-year-old to strep throat a few months ago?" she asked. She looked horrified. (You know the expression.)

"Yes," I replied, "but I think that I'm handling that okay. As well as can be expected anyway, but this thing at work is driving me crazy."

Tears trickled down her face. *Here we go again, everyone with the crying. I hate the crying.*

When she pulled it together, she explained that she had a

three-year-old grandson. She couldn't imagine such a loss. I thought, "No, you can't imagine it." I wasn't crying.

She looked at me. "You know you don't have to hold it together in here. You don't need to be strong in here. That's what I'm here for—for you, to help you."

I shrugged.

"How often do you cry about your son?" she asked.

"Not very often," I answered. "It doesn't do any good. Crying can't bring him back. Crying doesn't make me feel any better. Plus, it just makes my eyes hurt for the rest of the day. Crying is a waste of time, and I don't like it."

I saw tears in her eyes again. I was about to leave, but then she said something I must admit probably saved me from more time in the deepest part of the grief pit: "You're not losing your mind, Kim; it's called grieving. Grief will not be denied. Grief *will* come out. You can't simply set it aside. Grief must be experienced. It's a process. You can't think or remember because your grief is taking up all the space in your mind. You have to let it out, or it will come out in physical ways like you're experiencing."

I was shaking my head, fighting my tears now. I was sad-mad and glaring at her. She sensed my fear. I didn't think I could face this thing head on, look straight into the dark hole inside. I just wanted to fix it. Put something over it so I didn't have to look at it or feel it. It was difficult enough to stop that replay tape from playing in my mind, let alone deal with the reality of the rest of my life . . . without Austin.

"Can you tell me why you don't cry?" she asked.

"I already told you. It's a waste of time," I responded, and added a silent "duh!"

"You can't really believe that," she said. "Even if you do believe that, it's not the whole reason. Why else? Is it because you want to maintain the appearance of holding it together? You don't want anyone to perceive that you are weak? You seem like the type of woman who insists on holding it together, especially in front of other people."

I wondered how she nailed that on the head in thirty short minutes with me. I was shocked. She pegged me. I despised weepy, whining, emotional, or weak-minded anything in myself. I hate to admit it, but it annoyed me in others, too. I considered it attention-seeking. I tended to avoid "those" types of people. The weak were "energy vampires" to me. They sucked all my energy and positivity out. I was determined to be strong, courageous, capable of handling anything. You can count on me! Losing it in front of anyone was *not* an option for me.

"How about we try something this week and see how it goes?" she asked gently. I shrugged again, half-hearted this time. I was already exhausted just thinking about letting this grief out.

"I'd like you to make an appointment in your calendar to grieve," she said. "Select a time and a place where you can be completely alone for thirty minutes. Go to that place, and just be open to letting out whatever emotion comes. Don't stop it. Just let it out. When your time is up, get up and hold it together for the rest of the day. Deal?"

It sounded practical and not all "touchy-feely," so I agreed.

I thought about where I could go, where I wouldn't be embarrassed when the deep, ugly cry of my heart came out. It was difficult to think of a private spot because she told me my car was not a safe option unless it was parked somewhere. If I cried in a parked car somewhere, it would be my luck someone would probably knock on the window or call the cops.

No, my car was not an option. I finally selected a little dock on a pond inside our neighborhood. I could walk to it from our house. I would walk on the same sidewalks where I often took the boys. I would pass the park where we always played. I had no doubt that I would feel something that needed to be let out by the time I reached that dock.

She was right. I wasn't really grieving. I was stuffing it down inside. I was trying to "manage" my grieving process. Now, I know that resistance is futile. Grief will not be denied. Grief will happen.

Letting It Out

If you are trying to hold it together or are afraid of letting grief out, please be encouraged. The ocean of grief did not swallow me whole, never to return, like I thought it would. It did hurt me. But it didn't break me.

In fact, after a week or two of making my appointments to grieve, I started to be able to read and comprehend again (most of the time). It didn't happen all at once or right away, but slowly and over time my mind returned. Letting out the emotions surrounding losing Austin allowed my mind the

> Some days I sat in wonder at the nature around me, just letting beauty wash my wounds.

ability to process other things.

The constant replay of the images of Austin being worked on in that hospital popped up less. The feel of his skin cooling while he lay there in that hospital bed did not stop me in my tracks nearly as much. All the horrifying moments seemed to replay less when I spent time actually grieving and letting out the utter madness of that day. Since I was no longer stuffing the trauma deep down into my soul, it seemed to have less of a hold on me. Those replay moments began to subside, but I vowed to tell you the truth, so I must admit that there are times when "that day" flashes into my mind and takes my breath away all over again. Some things still trigger a rewind and replay of my worst day. Those moments, however, did become less and less as I allowed the reality of our loss to be expressed.

My appointments to grieve were filled with all types of emotions and behaviors. Some days, I let out the ugly cry and curled up into the fetal position on that dock. Some days, I sat while tears rolled down my face. Some days, I laughed at the funny things Austin did. Some days, I sat in wonder at the nature around me, just letting beauty wash my wounds. Some days, I threw rocks at God and people who let me down. Some days, I felt good sitting there.

Yes, some days I laughed. Some days I felt good. Some days my soul felt a bit of healing. It will happen, my friend. Maybe not right away and certainly not all the time. But, since God said He would be close to the brokenhearted (that's definitely us) and save us from being crushed in spirit (that's grief), He will. When grief feels its darkest, cry out to God. He will answer you.

Psalm 18 tells me so:

I love you, O LORD, my strength.

The LORD is my rock and my fortress and my deliverer,
my God, my rock, in whom I take refuge,
my shield, and the horn of my salvation, my stronghold.

I call upon the LORD, who is worthy to be praised,
and I am saved from my enemies.

The cords of death encompassed me;
the torrents of destruction assailed me;
the cords of Sheol entangled me;
the snares of death confronted me.

In my distress I called upon the LORD;
to my God I cried for help.
From his temple he heard my voice,
and my cry to him reached his ears.

He sent from on high, he took me;
he drew me out of many waters.
He rescued me from my strong enemy
and from those who hated me,

for they were too mighty for me.

They confronted me in the day of my calamity,
but the Lord was my support.
He brought me out into a broad place;
he rescued me, because he delighted in me.
(PSALM 18:1-6, 16-19)

When the replay won't stop in my mind, and panic begins to rise, I pray these verses:

Rejoice in the Lord always; again I will say, rejoice.
Let your reasonableness be known to everyone. The Lord
is at hand; do not be anxious about anything,
but in everything by prayer and supplication with
thanksgiving let your requests be made known to God.
And the peace of God, which surpasses
all understanding, will guard your hearts
and your minds in Christ Jesus.
(PHILIPPIANS 4:4-7)

These verses tell me to remember that I do have good things in my life (rejoice in the Lord). Next, to pray and make my requests known to God. The result is that God will guard my heart and my mind. When the flashbacks start, they start in your mind and then stop your heart. You need God to guard your heart *and* your mind. When a trigger jumps out at you unexpectedly, you can quickly pray to God and ask Him to guard your heart and your mind. Ask Him to make it stop.

Take action to make it stop by starting to give thanks to God for something, anything will do. Take charge of your mind. Don't let the darkness win it over. Instead, grab hold of something you are grateful for and shift your focus to crying out to God. Ask Him to fulfill His promise to guard your heart *and* your mind through Jesus. For example, whenever Ethan would sniffle, we would practically fall apart with worry. We didn't, however, want Ethan to have to deal with crazy parents in addition to not having his big brother. So we did our best to hide this particular "crazy" from him. Instead, I would thank God that Ethan was a strong and healthy child. I thanked God that Ethan was whole and happy. Next, I would beg the Lord to allow me to physically feel His presence around me, to be comforted and calmed. Requesting healing of whatever was bothering Ethan came next. Finally, I would remind God that He promised to fill me with peace beyond my comprehension and to guard my heart and mind (Phil. 4). I asked Him to keep those promises and allow me to feel differently right in that very moment, for worry about Ethan to decrease and for me to be able to be filled with peace.

Also, don't be afraid to ask for professional help in addition to your prayers. After working with my counselor, I also talked to my primary care doctor. In an effort to help me deal with the flashbacks and the anxiety, I was prescribed an anti-anxiety medication. While taking the medicine, I felt more like a grieving mom and less like I was going to lose my mind. I needed the anti-anxiety medicine for about six to eight months, and then my doctor helped me lessen the dosage until I was able to feel like myself without it.

For those of you who fear taking some medicine that alters your state of mind, may I tell you I felt the same way. I did not begin taking the medicine until about six months after Austin died because I was so resistant to taking medications to help me cope. I can assure you, however, that the medicine I took did not make me feel like I was taking something to alter my mental state. The medicine did not make me feel "loopy" or intoxicated. I didn't feel numb or tired. The medicine simply made me feel like *myself*, like my normal self, in the midst of losing our son. I'm very glad that I took it. The medicine was easy to wean off of. Nothing I was afraid of about taking medication happened to me. The medicine simply did its job of balancing my mind for a bit.

For those of you who might be discouraged by others, or have been told to avoid getting help by way of medication, I only ask one question: has that person ever lost a child? My guess is no. Please allow yourself to *at least* explore the options with a doctor and make your own decision. No one else must walk this ragged road but you. You get help where and when you need it. There's no shame in that or the process of grieving a child.

As we close this chapter of our journey together, know that I have cried along with you. I have been on my knees crying out to God. Remembering the first days of the loss of a child will never leave me . . . or you. We can only hope to manage those memories in a way that lets us continue to live this life while we wait on heaven. I pray the ideas below give you some tips or tools to stop the replay and manage the memories. Peace to you, my friend. May your mind be guarded at all times by God through Christ Jesus.

SURVIVAL STEP:
Let It Out

This survivor step is like peroxide for your soul. It's time to clean out that wound. It's going to hurt, but you must do it if you want to heal. Just like cleaning a cut or scrape on your skin, if you don't take care of it and clean it out, it will get infected. Your grief is the same. If you don't let it out, it will begin to seep out in other ways. As the saying goes, "Buck up, buttercup." It's time to get to work. Be aware that you will be physically and mentally exhausted during this step. That precious counselor I wrote about above told me another thing that helps me during the tough days:

> "If you crawled out of bed, got dressed, and brushed your teeth, you are doing great! Simply taking care of yourself and your basic daily tasks is enough for now. Stop acting like nothing happened and cut yourself some slack. Seriously, brushing your teeth should be considered a victory."

Now that I am out of the pit, and can see how deep and dark it really is, I must tell you that she was right. If you are merely functioning right now, you are doing great!

Try some of these "let it out" ideas, but then make sure to give yourself some extra slack on your life activities and roles. You'll need a little extra tender loving care during this phase. If you are good at letting friends help you, ask friends to come alongside you during this time. Ask for whatever you need to make life a bit easier: meals, care for other children, cleaning, groceries, etc.

If you are not someone who is good at asking for or receiving help (like me), then you must allow yourself grace and mercy. You may not be at your best, personally or professionally, for the next few months—and that's okay. Stop hyperventilating at that thought. Trust me because I've been there. Give yourself grace to grieve. You are not superhuman. You may be short-tempered, unfocused, emotional, etc. But don't avoid this step because it's not comfortable. Don't worry—your usual perfection-seeking self will return after she beats the stuffing out of grief!

Ideas:

- Make an appointment to grieve: thirty minutes every day.
- Take walks: let nature whisper into your heart.
- Smash some dishes: buy some $1 dishes at Goodwill or a thrift store, find a good place, and smash them to bits.

- Journal like no one's reading it: write all the ugly thoughts and feelings you have, and do not self-edit in case someone finds it. Write everything that comes to mind, no matter what.
- Find Bible verses that speak to your broken heart, and write them on post-it notes placed in a few trigger spots. Some verses that really helped me include Psalms 29:11, 34:18, 63:3; John 14:27, 16:22–33; Romans 15:13; Philippians 4:4–8; and Revelation 21:3–4.
- Go to the grave (or not): visit the site where your child is buried. This works for some, but *not* for me. I rarely go to Austin's grave, only once every couple of years (and that's okay, too).
- Look at pictures: make a small album of your favorite pictures of your child.
- Wear it out: wear or take an article of clothing that was your child's; I often wore my brother's jean jacket after he died in a car accident in 1989. It made me miss him so much, but it also made me feel close to him.
- See a counselor.
- See your primary care doctor.
- Ask two friends to pray specifically about your grieving process and stopping the replay for the next thirty days.

Choose at least one thing that digs at your soul and makes the grief feel like it's too much to handle. Remember, we are cleaning that wound by letting the hurt out as much as we can.

Please note that this is a gut-wrenching process, and

I highly recommend that you make sure to do some of the spiritual steps below. The spiritual steps will be like Neosporin for your soul!

SPIRITUAL STEP:
Turn to God

Trying to get through your grief without God is like taking medicine that only helps the symptoms of a disease. You need true healing, not temporary feel-good options. There are things you can try to ease your pain: alcohol, drugs, shopping, food, gambling, etc. These things or activities, however, are only temporary, and some of them are dangerous to you and others in your life.

The hole in your heart from losing your child is simply too big for the things of this world. You need something bigger, something better. You need the Healer. You need Jesus.

Jesus is the Neosporin for your soul. As you are cleaning out that wound by letting out your grief, you need something to soothe your soul. Your heart will be raw and painful. You'll need a healing balm to cover that wound.

I remember when the pain would hurt so badly I couldn't seem to breathe. I felt like it was difficult to catch my breath. I was always trying to sit up taller and take in more air. Sometimes, I would physically rub the spot over my heart and beg Jesus to do something to take some of the hurt away.

"Please, God," I would beg, "reach down into me and help me. This is too much. It's too much. Help me with this pain. It hurts so much. Please soothe it away, even just a little bit. Make it hurt less!"

And then I would take a deep breath, and usually, it did seem like it hurt less. My chest felt lighter. It felt like I could get a deep breath again. God is right beside you, my friend. Just turn to Him and ask Him to help you. You won't regret it.

Ideas:

- Put your trust in Jesus as your Lord and Savior. If needed, go back to page 34, and fall on your knees before God. Pray to accept Jesus as your Savior, and receive the gift of salvation.

- If you already know Jesus, remember you are a child of God. Lean into your Father in heaven, let Him wrap His arms around you, and pound your tiny fists against His mighty chest if you need to (He can take it!).

- Find a Bible and read the Gospel of John in the New Testament. A multitude of loving promises pour off those pages, especially regarding our relationship with God and eternal life. This was the book in the Bible that almost gave me my next breath at times.

- Call on Jesus as the Healer. While He was here on earth, Jesus healed the sick, made the blind see, made the lame walk, and even raised people from the dead. He can mend our broken hearts if we ask Him to help us.

- Put Scripture verses that speak of God's comfort or power in a place where you will see them. We have already mentioned several above; visit my website at KimAErickson.com for more verse ideas. Putting verses up where your trigger moments tend to happen is powerful.
- Ask two people to pray specifically for your relationship with God for the next thirty days.
- Find a church, or keep going to your church, so that you don't shut out other people who can help you work on your relationship with God during this time.

when everyone moves on

At some point, everyone will go home. They will stop delivering food. Visits will become less and less. This might be a relief to you, or it may strike you with panic. Either way, the time has come for you to face life without your child on your own as a family. Once the initial response is over, it might seem like people are avoiding you. You don't get invited to lunch. Backyard barbeques take place without you. Conversations seem to halt when you walk up.

My inward parts are in turmoil and never still;
days of affliction come to meet me.
I go about darkened, but not by the sun;
I stand up in the assembly and cry for help.
I am a brother of jackals
and a companion of ostriches.
(JOB 30:27–29)

At the time your grief is really hitting you the hardest, it may seem people around you have their heads in the sand like ostriches. Folks are unsure what to do once the time for casserole dishes and sympathy cards is over. They are not trying to hurt you. They just don't know what else to do to help you.

For me, this season was one of the most difficult. While I am an introvert at heart, the busyness of having people around kept me from focusing on the expanse of life that stretched before me without Austin. The peace and quiet, the "normal" of my household, was a relief in many respects, but it also came with the price of deep gashes of loneliness from missing my vibrant three-year-old. Often it felt as if my feet had been knocked out from under me again.

I went back to work about a week after Austin's funeral. I literally didn't know what else to do. I loved being at home with Ethan, but Miss Alma also needed to go back to her work of being our nanny. She struggled with only caring for Ethan and missing Austin. The giant hole of losing Austin only seemed to be getting bigger. The loneliness of realizing that I couldn't talk to Austin anymore was increased when I saw coworkers going out to lunch or chatting in the hallways. My family had gone back home and were back to work, too. Time kept turning, turning, turning, making me sick to my stomach.

Cement Shoes and Wet Blankets

This was the season of cement shoes and wet blankets. Each day it felt as if my feet were encased in heavy cement shoes.

There seemed to be a wet patch of cement on the floor on my side of the bed. The minute I got out of bed and tried to go to the bathroom, my feet felt heavy. It felt difficult to put one foot in front of the other. By the time I got dressed, I felt wrapped in one of those scratchy, heavy wool blankets that happened to be soaking wet. The blanket was difficult to manage all day long on top of those cement shoes. My grief seemed to add to the weight of my body and get caught on things as I moved about my day.

Of course, I didn't have cement shoes or a wet blanket wrapped around me, but my soul felt unbearably heavy and my heart would get tripped up several times throughout the day. While I was trying to work or do everyday things, it seemed my grief would well up and take me off task. It was like walking around with a blanket all day. Everyone was looking at the blanket and at me under it, wondering how I got through the day carrying my grief out in the open. The worst was when they would look at me, and I'd trip over that darn blanket and begin to cry. Ugh. It was not only exhausting, it was so annoying to me. I was trying to get back to "normal," but how could I with cement shoes and a wet blanket to carry while I worked?!

I wanted to ask people how they could go back to their normal lives when things were clearly out of hand around here. On the other hand, I wanted them to stop looking at me differently, treating me with delicacy, or pitying me. It was a tightrope of emotions with no end in sight. The good news is I didn't feel this season lasted as long as some others. It seemed like my mind and body got used to maneuvering through my day in cement shoes and carrying a wet blanket.

It may not seem like it now, but you will get through this part of your grief journey. Your grief right now feels heavy, unmanageable, and visible to others. But you will learn how to lift your feet up a bit more and how to avoid tripping over the blanket. This is the season where you learn how to get through one day at a time, slowly taking one careful step after another. After a while, those cement shoes wear down because you refused to give up walking. You eventually learn how to wrap that heavy grief blanket in such a way that it doesn't snag on the furniture of life all the time.

You *will* learn to manage your grief. You are correct in thinking that time will not help you. Losing a child is different from other losses. *This* wound *won't* heal with time. So, our goal is to get better at managing our grief.

Now that everyone has gone home, are there things around the house that you could put away or move to a more discreet spot? Do you notice that your sadness spikes when you enter a certain room in the house or office? Try to figure out what is triggering your grief. Ask yourself if there is something you could do to your home or office to lessen the sting of your grief.

For my husband and me, pictures of Austin were and are a major trigger. When we see his happy face, it makes us incredibly sad. For my mom, however, seeing my brothers' faces helps her remember that they were happy and that people will remember them in a positive way from their pictures. Austin's room, with his "hunnel" bed (he was trying to say "tunnel";

since it was a bunk bed, he thought it made a fun tunnel like the blanket over the couch and coffee table), caused both of us too much pain. Seeing his room each time we went up to Ethan's nursery was like entering a battleground. I would prepare my heart each time I tried to make my cement shoes go up the stairs to get Ethan from his crib. Relief would wash over me that Ethan was alive and healthy as pressure would rise in my chest because Austin's bed lay empty.

> This season was a mixed bag of trying to manage my grief and wanting to feel close to Austin.

We managed our grief early on by taking down the pictures and closing Austin's bedroom door. In my office, I took down pictures of Austin as well. I tucked them into drawers so I could get some work done, but I didn't put them far out of reach. I needed to be able to pull those pictures out when I felt so far away from my little boy that I couldn't bear one more minute. This season was a mixed bag of trying to manage my grief and wanting to feel close to Austin.

You may find that managing your grief is a tug-of-war with your need to keep your child's things close. Lowering the number of times your grief gets triggered in a day is in direct conflict with the cry of your heart. You don't want to ever forget what his voice sounded like. Her smile is something you can't imagine living without. Your heart clings to every memory, big and small, like your life depends on always being able to pull those moments to your mind. How will you do both? How will you be able to go forward with your life and hold your child in your mind's eye, knowing she will never return?

It may seem impossible right now. I know it did to me. I could not imagine how I was going to cling to Austin's memories *and* do the normal things of every day. It seemed too painful to do both because I did not want daily life to exist without Austin. When I started making an effort to remove my triggers, however, it seemed like a path opened up before me. I felt more in control, more in charge, of the raging beast inside that is grieving a child. When I put photographs in drawers, I could decide if I needed to pull them out and see his face. With his bedroom door closed, I could wait until Ethan was in bed before I went in that "hunnel" bed and cried myself silly.

Remember, this is no one's loss but yours. No one else is the mom. Only you. While the loneliness of this fact seems too heavy to bear right now, grab hold of the control your status as "mom" offers. If you need to keep things the same in order to feel less anxious, then things stay put. Period. If you need to change a room, put things away, or even move out of a house or office, then do it. Period. End of discussion. The only person you need to check in with is the child's father. He has the same giant hole in his heart as you do. The dad is entitled to this same, wide latitude in choices. I pray you will both be on the same "page," or at least be able to reach a common ground where both of your triggers can be lessened as much as possible.

Please keep in mind that as you learn to manage your grief,

you are learning a new skill. You may try things that don't work. You may step on some people's feelings. In addition, you may not be able to handle many other things as you tackle this new skill. Managing your grief may be all that you are capable of during this time. Remember when my counselor said that getting up and brushing your teeth should be considered a victory? This mindset still applies during this season.

Give yourself some extra time to complete tasks. Don't take on things that would have stressed you out before your child passed away. Extra stress is not what you need right now. You need some time to settle into life without your child. New life skills are necessary right now. As a "rookie" in this grieving process, you need extra time for tasks and a wide road for mistakes. Surround yourself with people who are encouraging to you. Tell people what you are trying to do. It might help them feel less awkward around you.

As for people avoiding you, you likely need to make the first step. Smile at folks, let them know you are open to conversation. Ask someone to lunch. Take the kids to the park and strike up conversation. Even as I type this, I am powerfully aware of how difficult this will be for you.

Doing social settings and making conversation are *still* some of the most difficult things for my husband and me. The shallowness of conversation and the amount of complaining that takes place in most social settings feels so unimportant when you've lost a child. These thoughts might run through your mind: Don't they know your child died? How could they complain about their kids? Don't they know they could lose a child at any moment? Why are we talking about football when that won't save another child from cancer? Who cares? Who cares about . . . anything . . .

You get the idea. Going back to life as you knew it is not likely. That backyard barbeque or lunch with your girlfriends will not feel the same for a very long time, if ever. But you must eat, and you must socialize with other humans (kind of . . . we do a lot less nowadays). You likely have to go back to work, either in the home or outside the home. Either way, work needs to be completed, and other humans will touch aspects of that work. Interacting with others may be one of the most difficult new skills you must acquire. While both my husband and I were very social before, it seemed like grinding our teeth after Austin died.

Perhaps it was this difficulty making conversation or being social that led others to avoid us or act like ostriches. Perhaps it wasn't *them* at all, but *us*. Perhaps I was the first to stick my head into the sand. I can see it now, but at the time, it simply felt frustrating to see others interacting like nothing happened. It was painful to know that their lives simply went on as before Austin died. Nothing was out of place for the people around me. Everything was out of place for me.

Learning to live with everything out of place is what you must do now. You'll need new strategies and creative ideas to hold it together. I hope some of the ideas below work for your transition into life without your precious child.

SURVIVAL STEP:
Learn to Manage Your Grief

You can go ahead and scream it now: "I DON'T WANT TO LEARN TO LIVE WITHOUT MY CHILD!" I know. I remember. I still don't want to deal with losing Austin. I want to never feel the loss of him again. Yet, it still happens to me. Every. Single. Day. Even ten years later. Our reality stinks. Our lives must go on because we have no other choice. We are here, waiting for what seems like eternity, to see our child again. No amount of life skills or strategies are going to change our miserable hearts. I'm so sorry for that reality, but you don't have another option but to try to live your life to the best of your abiliy. There are people around you who love you so much. They still need you. You have things to handle on this earth, people who love you, and responsibilities to carry on. There's only one you, and you are important. I pray these ideas get you started and help you begin to live while you grieve.

Ideas:

- Look around your house (and office) and ask yourself if anything specific seems to be triggering deep grieving moments.
- Consider putting pictures in more discreet areas of the house, where you won't see them several times a day— or, just the opposite, consider placing pictures where

you can see the face of your child each day; whatever works for you.

- Think about the activities you do on a regular basis that trigger major breakdowns; consider whether you can change the activity, change the location, do something different, or ask for help doing that activity.
- Make your "to-do" list, and see if you can delegate anything to those folks who've offered to help.
- Say "not right now" to anything you think would add stress to your life, even if you would have been able to handle it before; if it seems like too much right now, it probably is.
- Keep that appointment and special place to grieve. Even as you transition back to your regular routine, you'll need to keep letting the grief out.
- Find books to read that take your mind to a different place—a world of fantasy, perhaps, or exploring new intellectual concepts. Escape the weight of that grief blanket for a while.
- Exercise! If exercise was part of your routine before your child died, you'll likely be craving it by now; if exercise wasn't part of your regular routine, consider adding a brisk walk three or four times a week. Getting your heart rate up will battle against those cement shoes.
- Keep your self-care at a high level; rest when you need it, eat well, take a bubble bath, lunch with a friend, get a massage.

- Give yourself an extra day or two on any deadlines or tasks that need to be completed.
- Feeling tired is normal, but don't hesitate to seek medical or counseling help if you wonder if you might be falling into depression.
- Put encouraging pictures or inspiring sayings around your daily area to remind you that you are on a difficult journey, but *not* at a hopeless dead end or in a never-ending loop; you will get better at managing your pain.
- Pets can be wonderfully therapeutic. I don't have a dog but have heard from others in grief that a dog, cat, or even a bird can offer companionship, comfort, and (with a dog) a reason to get out and walk!

SPIRITUAL STEP:
Start Your Day Talking with God

As you attempt to step back into some sort of regular routine, you will need the help of God to get through the most mundane of days. Developing coping mechanisms for your grief will be easier if you cry out to God for help. Since you are in the process of developing a new "normal" anyway, you should try to develop a morning chat with God. You can call it prayer time if you want, but it can also be a simple talk with God. Don't worry about doing something "right" because your heavenly Father only cares for your heart and your pain. He wants to hold you in His mighty arms and give you comfort.

There really is no right or wrong way to pray. Just try talking to Him like He is sitting at your kitchen table. As you start your day, what concerns you? What worries you? Is there a specific pain in your heart today? Grieving the loss of a child has so many different angles and perspectives. What stabs at your heart each morning can change and shift like sand. Go ahead and tell God what is hurting you on this particular day.

Ask God to give you ideas to help decrease the pain. Ask God to take the crushing weight of this loss from you. Ask Him to carry around that heavy blanket of grief today, to help make sure your grief doesn't get tangled up with your tasks for the day.

Beg God for strength to get through the day. One day at a time. Plead for the Almighty to intervene and lift some of grief's burden each day. Ask the Father to shelter you from more pain today. Request understanding and patience for those who might encounter you under your grief today. Pray for patience for yourself as you learn these new skills of managing unimaginable grief.

Ideas:

- Give yourself fifteen extra minutes each morning to talk with God.
- Try to set aside any restraints or rules you may think apply to prayer. Just talk to God. He knows what's in your head and heart already, so you might as well say it

to Him directly. Remember, He can take whatever you dish out.

- Get the book *Grieving the Loss of a Loved One: A Devotional of Comfort as You Mourn* by Kathe Wunnenberg. Written by a mom who has lost a child, the book includes short daily readings to help you find peace; use the daily reading or Scriptures to start your conversation with God.

- Get the *Streams in the Desert* devotional book by L. B. Cowman and James Reimann. It has short daily readings about living through suffering, and it may help you feel less alone to read about others who have walked the suffering streets before you.

- Consider journaling your thoughts; write as though you are talking to God. Don't self-edit this writing, no one will read it but you.

- Read the Psalms. When you find one that touches your heart or speaks to your grief, read it out loud, and let that start your conversation with God. Tell Him why or how you feel a certain way; ask Him to fulfill the promises you read in Psalms. Some psalms that have really comforted me include Psalms 18, 22, 23, 39, 69, 91, 102, 103, 107, 116, 121, 130, and 143.

- Listen to Christian music if you have difficulty getting any words out; let the songs speak for you when you can't string two words together (it happens and it's okay). I have created a playlist that's on my website at KimAErickson.com.

dealing with others

I'm sure people have said the most awful stuff to you already. Comparing the loss of their dog to losing your child. Saying how they know how you feel because they lost their beloved grandmother ten years ago (not that losing your grandma isn't a big deal; it just isn't the same as losing your child). It would have been better for those folks to say nothing at all or just "I'm sorry." The reality is that we have to deal with others as we are muddling through this unfathomable pain.

We might wish they could be more like these three:

Now when Job's three friends heard of all this evil that had come upon him, they came each from his own place. . . . They made an appointment together to come to show him sympathy and comfort him. And when they saw him from a distance, they did not recognize him. And they raised their voices and wept, and they tore their robes

and sprinkled dust on their heads toward heaven.
And they sat with him on the ground seven days
and seven nights, and no one spoke a word to him,
for they saw that his suffering was very great.
(JOB 2:11–13)

When I read the verses above in my Bible I thought, "YES! that's exactly what I needed!" I just needed my friends to sit with me, to be there. It was okay if they were silent. It was okay if they just passed the tissues. There were no words anyone could have said that would have lifted my misery. Even today, words cannot ease the heartbreak of losing a child.

But we have to deal with others, for better or worse. And in our grief we don't always get it right. I know that I hurt people in this season by my responses, or more accurately, my lack of any responses. I had a difficult time responding to the beautiful things my friends and coworkers did for me. I just didn't have the energy. I just couldn't muster the care, about anything. It was all I could do to function, let alone do the socially proper thing or even have polite manners in response to an act of kindness. Sometimes I remembered, but sometimes I would forget.

Deeply harbored feelings of anger and resentment swelled inside me when faced with others who were trying to enter into my grief with me. If a person who didn't have a friendship with me suddenly wanted to talk about how I was doing, I wanted to reach out and push them away. We didn't have conversations about how I was doing in life before Austin died, and *now* you want to enter my personal pain and find out how I'm doing? I felt it was really coming from either a place of gossip or a desire to call herself/himself a friend of mine because I was getting a lot of attention at home and at work. Actually, I have no idea why people would insert themselves into your grief when they've had no place in your heart or your life before. Yet, they did it to me and I'm betting folks are doing it to you as well.

At this point, I can look back and have more compassion or empathy for those folks. I can give them the benefit of the doubt. Perhaps my loss moved them, and their heart really did initiate the sudden concern. At the time, however, kind thoughts did not run through my mind, and I really did want to slap them upside the head! If you are feeling the same way, just know you aren't alone, and try your best to walk away.

Dealing with my friends was a whole different matter. I don't even remember much about interacting with my friends for the first year after Austin died. Maybe that's because I really *didn't* interact with them. I know that I failed to return texts and emails. Like A LOT. It hurt some friendships, at least for the time being. Phone calls? Forget it. It was as if talking required taking on 40 pounds of dead weight.

Talking to others remains difficult for me. And small talk with people I don't know very well? Dreadful! I'm not sure why conversations are so much more difficult now, but I do know that many others who've lost a child experience the same difficulty. A dear woman on my first book launch team (Kathleen Bailey Duncan, coauthor of *God's Healing in*

Grief, a Bible study to help you through the process) asked if I wanted to join a Facebook group, While We're Waiting, which is exclusively for parents who've lost children. It's a safe place to communicate with others who might understand the darkness of your thoughts and feelings, a place without judgment or hurt feelings. Soon after I joined the group, I realized how many parents would post a question or thought like these: Why is talking to people so hard? Small talk is impossible now! I can't seem to hold a conversation because I just don't care about whatever they are talking about. And on and on it went. Hundreds of people saying, "Me too!" or "It's okay, I am that way now, too."

While I don't post very often in that group, when I feel confused about my reaction to things, or just feel lonely in my loss of Austin, I get on that page and poke around. I can usually find someone who wrote about what I'm feeling. Then, I can see all the comments come streaming in, verifying that I am not alone in whatever thoughts or feelings are grabbing me that day. It makes me feel as "normal" as I can be while I walk this ragged road of grief.

I needed more empathy for others who were willing to enter my circle of pain.

If you'd like to join this Facebook group, I would be happy to recommend you and get you added to the group. It's a closed group to make sure privacy and understanding are kept at a high level. Let me know if you want to join While

We're Waiting on Facebook. Go to KimAErickson.com, use the "Contact Kim" form, and I'll see that you get set up. You will feel supported and understood among others who are walking a similar road.

Acknowledging that others are doing the best they can is something I wish that I could rewind and do better. I needed more empathy for anyone who was willing to enter my circle of pain and engage in my dark pit of grief. Anyone who talks to you right now, or early in your loss, is brave, very brave. It is not easy to stand next to someone who has just lost a child. Grief is uncomfortable at best. Whoever is willing to sit next to you in the dirt after you lose a child is a true friend—that friend who is willing to hear you out and be with you through all your emotions.

If you read the book of Job in your Bible, you'll see that Job's friends messed it up, too. Although their initial response, to show up and sit with Job in his grief, was amazing, their next efforts to "comfort" him involved telling Job he lost all ten of his children in one day because Job must have sinned against God. I remember feeling this way, like losing Austin was my fault, but I would not have responded well if one of my friends said such a thing to my face. Job didn't take it lying down either! God also scolded those friends for speaking wrongly about Him.

The bottom line is that someone close to you is likely to hurt your feelings during this time of grief. First, they don't know how to handle this pain any better than you do. Second, you are not in your right mind. Third, they are grieving, too.

Their grief is not to the level of your pain, but they have suffered a loss as well. Plus, they are watching you go through this nightmare. It's not easy, and I wish that I could rewind the clock and do the family and friend relationships better. I wish I had told them what I needed more specifically, even saying, "Please just sit with me quietly as I'm too exhausted to talk or tell you what I need" or "Please help me tell all the people coming over that I am not able to have so many people in my home right now and just to pray for me."

Another thing you'll notice is that your reactions likely will remain different for a long time. I feel as though my reactions are still "stuck" sometimes. I simply do not respond to family and friends like (I think) they hope I will react. For example, a cheerful "Merry Christmas!" or "I can't wait for _____'s birthday this year because we are going to Disney!" can still sucker-punch me. I try to smile and give back a cheerful response, but my heart hurts and my smile doesn't reach my eyes. I don't ask any follow-up questions. I don't seem excited for them or their family. Sometimes I can fake it pretty well, but sometimes I just can't. My dreams and hopes for my own family feel like broken glass in my heart. It doesn't happen all the time, but it happens often enough to include in this survival guide. Remember, I said I would tell you the truth. The truth is my heart is still broken, and sometimes my family and friends stomp on the cracks without knowing it.

On the opposite end of the spectrum, it was not only the excitement of those around me that chaffed my wound. Complaining really split it open. More, it made my mind explode!

How could anyone complain around me?! I was outraged by anyone with the gall to complain about anything in my presence. Righteous indignation filled my heart and mind. In the face of losing a child, everything else paled in comparison. But, you see, there was my mistake: comparison. I didn't like it when others compared their difficulties to mine. Yet, there I sat on my high horse doing the exact same thing. Surely, my loss was so much "more" than whatever they faced.

It's somewhat true, but altogether unfair. Yes, loss of a child is beyond whatever threshold of pain someone can imagine. That pain, however, doesn't lessen the trials or pain that others go through. You and I will carry this unique pain for the rest of our days here on earth. God has entrusted us with a tremendous responsibility. If we can handle *this* loss with His grace and love, then what inspiration, what light, can we shine for others? Our grief is, indeed, a huge cross to bear, a burden unlike any other. It's a bit like being the most talented athlete on a team. If the most naturally talented person on a team doesn't lead, it seems the whole team struggles. The naturally talented have a responsibility to show others how to work hard, to contribute to the team, to press on for excellence. When the most talented player leads, the whole team follows, in awe of him.

You and I, my friend, are walking a journey most parents fear more than anything else. If we can struggle through the broken glass of our hearts, if we can continue to crawl toward God, crying and bleeding still, then others will follow us. They will be in awe of our faith, our strength. Others will watch us and be led to the cross, to faith in Jesus. The loss of our children is our cross to bear, but Jesus placed it lovingly on our backs—so we can bravely bear its weight.

Lovingly? Bravely? Please, don't fling this book across the room or into the trash can just yet. You may not be ready for this understanding, and that's okay. It's understandable if you are still questioning God, angry at God. But, I pray you will eventually enter a place of rest and peace with God. A place where you recognize and feel God's deep love *for you*.

Please give yourself grace to mess things up along the way. The road is more steep and dangerous than we imagined, isn't it? Even in their darkest fears, others can't quite grasp the pain of losing a child. They might be able to understand the initial shock of it, but they cannot comprehend the length and depth of this trial, and *that's* where we can try our best to keep our eyes on God and focused on eternal life in heaven. In the pit of grief is where we have the opportunity to let the light of God shine and help others out of the darkness.

Dealing with others will be challenging and rewarding. You will face your ups and downs with family and friends. Just try your best to muster up some empathy and compassion for those beyond your close circles. They know not what they do! Try your best to give them grace and forgiveness if they hurt you, which they most certainly will. Since we are "cracked" already, it's not difficult for others to offend us and hurt us. Try to remember you are broken and they are too. Take deep breaths, and keep crawling toward the Light.

SURVIVAL STEP:
Prepare Yourself

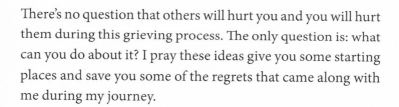

There's no question that others will hurt you and you will hurt them during this grieving process. The only question is: what can you do about it? I pray these ideas give you some starting places and save you some of the regrets that came along with me during my journey.

Ideas:

- Early on, ask one of your friends to handle responding to telephone calls, emails, inquiries, well-wishers, visitors, etc.
- Warn your family and friends ahead of time that you are tired, cranky, devastated, etc., and straight up ask for some grace and mercy if you say things you don't mean or if you fail to respond.
- Put a different message on your voicemail and email that thanks people for touching base, for caring about you, but that also lets people know you may not be responding to messages for a while.
- When you go back to work, prepare yourself for people stopping you in the hallway, in the breakroom, in the restroom (for crying out loud!) and asking how you are doing; perhaps prepare a prerecorded message that is filled with more graciousness than you might be feeling.

- Think of answers to these two questions each day: 1) How are you doing? and 2) Do you need anything? Make them up. Tell people something, anything, but prepare yourself to answer these two questions several times each day.
- Practice deep breathing as people approach you.
- Put up a quick prayer as people approach you: "God, please help me respond in a way that is pleasing to You and brings You glory."
- Say, "They are brave" each time someone comes to visit you.
- Repeat, "They are a good friend" each time a friend shows up for a while at your house.
- Remember that grief is uncomfortable for everyone.
- Ask for compassion for others even though you are the one crawling through glass.

SPIRITUAL STEP:
Try the Bible

Even if the Bible never made sense to you before, even if you are skeptical about the Bible, I encourage you to make Jesus your Lord and Savior, ask the Holy Spirit to help you, and try reading your Bible again. Why? Let me share what happened to me. I never thought much about the Bible before Austin died, other than that it seemed confusing and boring. I didn't like it at all. I tossed it aside.

After inviting Jesus into my life and heart as Lord, as Savior, His indwelling Holy Spirit came to me, and the Bible suddenly changed. Not kidding. I know it may sound strange to you. Believe me, if I had heard these statements before Austin died, I would have smiled and walked away (and rolled my eyes behind your back). I was so skeptical and unbelieving about the Bible. I thought white men wrote it thousands of years ago and that it couldn't possibly relate to me or my life, or most people's lives. "Bible-thumpers" made me think of the narrow-minded and perhaps uneducated.

Then, it happened to me. After I said, "I believe in Jesus. I believe He died to save me from my sins so I can have eternal life," the Bible became totally different to me. I didn't expect that to happen. In fact, I approached it like a challenge: let's just see if that preacher is right. . . . The pastor of the church I began attending after Austin's funeral said that when you accept the gift of Jesus for your salvation, you also get the gift of the Holy Spirit. Now, I thought, God will strike this man down right here in my kitchen! I thought the Holy Spirit was the power of God. Period. A lowly human didn't dare claim power or part of the Holy Spirit. That was God's thing. What was this guy all about? Had I joined a cult?! I planned to find out for myself.

The pastor's sweet wife treated me to coffee soon after Austin's funeral and answered my hundreds of questions about God, Jesus, heaven, and the Bible. She told me to start reading my Bible in the Gospel of John. I did.

You could have knocked me over with a feather. Holy cow! It made sense. I read faster. It touched my heart. I read more. It touched even the broken places in my heart. It eased my pain. I knew that I would never put it down again. If these words could pour a healing balm over this broken and bleeding mama heart, I'd clutch onto it for the rest of my life. I have. I will.

So grab a Bible. I dare you! First, however, I encourage you to believe and confess that Jesus is your Savior. I believe the Word of God does not have the same power without the gift of the Holy Spirit to help you hear and understand the words. Also, find someone to answer your questions as you read it. Get connected with a church that teaches from the Bible on Sundays. Someone there can help you. Some parts will still confuse you. Other parts will make you question what you thought was true. It's quite a journey on its own, let alone when read by a grieving and broken heart.

If you don't have a Bible (I didn't either; Austin's first nanny, Meghen, gave me one), you can go to my website (KimAErickson.com) and use the "Contact Kim" form, and I'd be happy to send one to you. If you decide to run to a bookstore to pick one up, beware—there are several versions. I would recommend an easy-to-read translation. The King James Version might be the one you remember with all of the "thee" and "thou" words, like the Shakespeare you didn't care to understand. I like the New American Standard Bible (NASB). The English Standard Version (ESV) and New International Version (NIV) are popular as well.

Ideas:

- Get an easy-to-read Bible. Start in the Gospel of John—a chapter a day is a great start.

- Read one psalm each day. You'll feel the pain and sorrow in those verses, but often the author ends by pointing to God and His comfort and power.

- Get connected with a small group and/or a person who can answer your questions.

- Talk to God before you begin reading; ask Him to give you a heart to read the Bible and a mind to understand it.

- Write down your thoughts and questions when you are finished reading.

- Talk to God after you finish reading and writing; ask Him to reveal the answers, to heal your broken heart, to make His presence known to you.

- Use your devotionals (see previous chapter where I recommended several, including *Grieving the Loss of a Loved One: A Devotional of Comfort as You Mourn* by Kathe Wunnenberg and *Streams in the Desert* by L. B. Cowman) to look up the verses referenced in the daily pages, especially if the daily reading spoke to your heart.

what to do
with stuff

If you are very early in your loss journey, I encourage you to avoid making any decisions right now that you do not absolutely have to make regarding your child's things. There are so many things. Shoes, clothes, sheets, pillows, awards, drawings, toys, books . . . all the favorite things that were his. The treasures that were hers alone. So much *stuff*.

Dealing with your child's stuff will likely be one of the most difficult steps you must take on this grief journey. It feels like salt in the wound. The wound still feels fresh and raw, but now you must decide what parts of your child's life you want to keep. It's unimaginable. Yet, you must. This is another thing that I cannot spare you from along our way. For the good of your healing and the healing of your family, at some point, you simply must go through the stuff that piles up in our lives.

Each piece may feel special to you now that your child is gone. In the back of your mind, in some tiny, rational place, you know that you probably won't keep everything forever. So, what do you do with all of the things that connect to your child?

> For the good of your healing and the healing of your family, at some point you simply must go through the stuff that piles up in our lives.

In chapter 1, you read that we created different storage bins for Austin's things. Some things you keep, some things you store for a while, and some things can be given away. There might be other items that you distribute to your family. When my brother Jeff died in a car accident in 1989, my immediate family gathered one day in his room. We went through each item, one at a time. Mom would pull it out of the closet or drawer, and someone would shout out, "I want that. I remember the day we picked out that jacket . . . " Our parents kept a few items, and each of us grabbed a few things to remember Jeff. We laughed a bit, cried a lot. I have no idea what happened to the remaining items, but I'm certain my mom would know if I asked her today, even all these years later.

Which leads me back to something I wrote earlier: this loss is yours alone. Only my mom and dad would remember what they did with my brother's things decades ago. Even though I lost my twenty-three-year-old brother when I was nineteen, and even though he was my closest sibling in age (and with whom I had the most memories at the time), that sibling loss was *not* like losing a child. Losing a child, especially a young child, is uniquely set apart to the parents and the parents alone. No one else can quite comprehend the magnitude of the pain that is the loss of a child. Your whole world is tipped upside down, and it never quite rights itself. Never.

As a result, as the parent, only you should decide what to do with your child's things. You also get to decide *when* to change, move, store, or give away those things you associate with your child. I wonder if you feel like these decisions are a huge weight that's been added to the already impossible burden of grief. I remember feeling overwhelmed and incompetent, incapable of thinking straight or making decisions. I was unsure of myself. I certainly didn't want to be deconstructing Austin's room, his toys, our home. I didn't want to remove the pieces of Austin that remained throughout our home.

Yet I knew deep in my soul that we had to do it. We had to deal with Austin's things so that we could move past the denial our hearts desired. Also, some things needed to be changed so that the replay would not happen over and over and over again. My husband and I had different triggers for the replay, so we had to communicate with each other in order to minimize the replay, but also honor the other parent's need to hold on to something. Hence, the bins. If something needed to come down or move out of daily eyesight, we had the bins to put items into without fear of losing treasured items.

At the time Austin died, we had to choose an outfit and whatever else we wanted buried with him. We chose his favorite pajamas, his boo (blanket), and woof-woof (favorite stuffed dog). I remember my sister stopping me as we packed up these things for the funeral home.

"Are you sure you want to let go of Austin's blanket and his doggy?" she asked me. "Are you sure you want to bury them?"

"Of course!" I replied (rather sharply, I regret), looking at her like she had three heads.

"But, honey, you might want to have those things around later, for you or for Devin, maybe Ethan," my sister said gently.

"They're his favorites," I said through gritted teeth, tears sliding down my face.

She let it go. I wish I had listened to her. Now, so many years later, I wish we had his baby blanket and that silly stuffed dog.

If you are nearly blinded by pain and still sick to your stomach, it's probably too early to make decisions about your child's things (unless they need to be moved to stop the replay; then into a bin they go). Remember that your child needs nothing right now. Austin didn't need his blanket or woof-woof. He was *more* than fine, up in heaven, with no earthly needs or wants. If you are unsure whether something should be given away, I humbly encourage you to keep it for a while.

As for Austin's room, we kept it the same for several months. Ethan loved to play on the bunk beds, and it just didn't feel right to change his room right away. At some point, it became clear that my husband (who had grabbed Austin from that bed and started CPR) could not stop the horror in his mind if we didn't do something. I wasn't ready to move out of the house, although I think Devin would have left it in a split-second. All my memories of Austin were in that house. Every. Single. One.

Painting Over Austin's Fingerprints

Instead of moving, we agreed to redo Austin's room into a playroom. It must have been around Christmas that same year (so about eight months after Austin died) that we donated all the furniture to a family who needed it. The law firm I worked for always did a huge Christmas delivery to several families in the city. I remember colleagues coming over to pick up Austin's bedroom furniture for the Christmas delivery. Everyone was trying desperately to hold it together while we carried everything out and loaded it into someone's truck.

> As you grieve your child, you will find that your heart can break over and over again.

Devin, however, did not help. I think he took Ethan and did something else that night. That room, that furniture, *those* memories were simply too much for his heart and his mind. I say this to point out that your feelings might be different from your spouse's (or your child's other parent). These are rough waters to navigate. Each memory is highly charged. Each parent is clinging, mentally hanging on by a thread. Let me encourage you to express to the other parent *why* you want to move, keep, store, or give away your child's things. Your communication will be key to getting through the grieving process with the least amount of relationship damage possible.

After the furniture was gone, Devin's parents came from

Florida to Arizona to help us redo the room. We painted it a new color and made one wall a chalkboard. We hung new things on the walls. I distinctly remember when I had to paint over Austin's fingerprints on the wall where his bed used to be located. Oh, how I didn't want to do it. I wanted to sit right there on the floor and just stare at the last little bit of him in that room! It was excruciating to redo Austin's room, but it was best for Devin and for baby Ethan. It was best for our family's healing.

Several years later, it became clear that moving entirely out of that house and neighborhood were necessary for us to keep healing. The housing market had crashed, so we decided to rent our house. My job had changed as well, and we were able to transfer my job to Jacksonville, Florida. For several weeks before the big move, Devin held garage sales, and we let *everything* go, except for the "Austin's—Keep" bins, our beds, and a box or two of treasured family items.

The purge was so healing for us. As we drove away in that moving van, however, my heart broke again. All of my hopes and dreams began and ended in that house. It just wasn't fair. The finality of Austin's death washed over me anew. As you grieve your child, you will find that your heart most certainly *can* break over and over again. As you heal, you'll take next steps, and some of those steps will feel like you are being crushed in the pit of grief again.

The bit of good news is that our God will lift you out of that pit time after time. Every time you feel yourself falling, scraping, dropping . . . you need only cry out to God, and His mighty hand will rescue you every time. Remember, God "is near to the brokenhearted and saves the crushed in spirit" (Ps. 34:18). When you're ready, you can keep repeating this promise as you sift through your child's things and decide what to keep and what to give away. I pray that you would feel the presence of God's comfort as you do the most unfathomable task.

SURVIVAL STEP:
Ask for Help

If an item of your child's is causing the horrible details of his or her death to replay in your mind, tell your spouse (or the child's other parent(s) if your family is blended) and ask if it can be moved to a safe place. When you feel ready to consider going through your child's things, tell them again. It's important that everyone be on the same page, as much as possible. I'm so grateful Devin allowed me to have those first couple of years in that house. On the flip side, looking back, I wish that I would have been more sensitive to his healing and his pain. I couldn't see out of my own pit to recognize the depth of his replay horrors. Please communicate! Tell each other how you feel about your child's things. Do what you can with what you have in common. Make a plan to revisit the rest in thirty days. Keep checking in with each other to see if "it's time."

Ideas:

- Get different bins: keep, store, give away.
- Consider whether something is triggering your replay; if so, move it out of sight for a while.
- Ask others if anything is triggering them; move the item out of sight for a while (keep it in your car, office, or purse if you need to see it).
- Consider donating to a specific family. Churches or social-service organizations can help identify those in need. It helped me so much to know that Austin's fun bunk beds and dresser were going to a family just getting out of a domestic violence situation. They had twin boys with no beds at all, and having that furniture was like winning the lottery for them. They sent pictures of the family looking so happy; it put a little healing balm on my mama heart.
- Ask for help. Get your support circle to do a first round of sorting: clothes in one pile, books in another, toys in another, etc. As they do the sorting, they can also look for what items should be thrown away vs. donated (stains, tears, broken items). They probably could do a pretty good job of making a "keep" pile as well. Remember, it's just a first round and you get to look at everything and make the final decision; you have veto power!
- Take pictures of some items you want to remember but also think might be passed on to bless another family.

- Ask other family members and friends if they want to go through the giveaway pile. Austin's nanny chose a few things, and his first nanny from when he was a baby held on to a couple of items. While this loss is uniquely yours, others are hurting and could use a reminder or token as well.

SPIRITUAL STEP:
Remember This Life Is Temporary

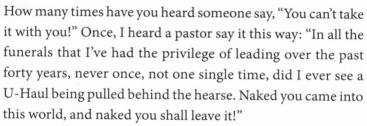

How many times have you heard someone say, "You can't take it with you!" Once, I heard a pastor say it this way: "In all the funerals that I've had the privilege of leading over the past forty years, never once, not one single time, did I ever see a U-Haul being pulled behind the hearse. Naked you came into this world, and naked you shall leave it!"

The pastor was quoting from Job in that last sentence. After Job lost everything, including all ten of his children, he fell to the ground and said, "Naked I came from my mother's womb, and naked shall I return. The LORD gave, and the LORD has taken away; blessed be the name of the LORD" (Job 1:21). The next verse goes on to say that "in all this Job did not sin or charge God with wrongdoing" (1:22).

I am certainly not claiming that I didn't sin in my grief because I am no Job! It's okay if you don't feel that way either. Folks who might say, "you just need to trust God" and imply that you should somehow find a way to be fine with losing your child have not read the rest of Job!

Job questioned God. Job asked, "Why me?" and felt like God didn't see him anymore. Job thought it would have been better if he hadn't been born in the first place. Job was hurt by the way others were treating him. Job wanted to go back to his life before he lost his kids.

Anyone else? I think part of the reason all of Job's feelings are recorded in our Bible is so we can see that even the most upright, God-fearing man had all of these responses to losing his children and suffering other hardships. Yet, when God answered Job (can you imagine?!), He didn't condemn Job for his feelings. God did put Job in his proper place: human, made by the will of God, created by the hand of God, breathed into existence by the Almighty. God responded by saying:

"Whatever is under the whole heaven is mine."
(JOB 41:11)

This reminder is one of the ways I keep my mind focused on heaven. Nothing here on earth belongs to me, not even Austin. This concept even keeps me from freaking out about Ethan. Ethan doesn't belong to me either. Even my children belong to God. Everything that happens here is only temporary, short, and pale in comparison to what is coming. Heaven is waiting. I'll take nothing from this world into heaven. Not even my "Austin's—Keep" bin.

Nothing but my heart will appear before the Almighty.

And as I look back from heaven into my time on earth, I will realize just how short and temporary it really was. Life on earth is tiny, microscopic even, in the face of eternity in a place with no more tears, no more pain, and no more death (Rev. 21:1–7).

I like the following three verses to remind me that this life on earth is temporary and the burden of our grief will soon be gone:

*Yet you do not know what tomorrow will bring.
What is your life? For you are a mist that appears
for a little time and then vanishes.*
(JAMES 4:14)

*Behold, you have made my days a few handbreadths,
and my lifetime is as nothing before you.
Surely all mankind stands as a mere breath!*
(PSALM 39:5)

*Man is like a breath; his days are like
a passing shadow.*
(PSALM 144:4)

Ideas:

- Write some of these verses on post-it notes, and place them in spots you see every day.

- Look for pictures online that make you think of heaven; post those around you as well.
- When you look around at all your child's things, remember that those items didn't go with him or her into the eternal life; that stuff sat right here on earth, not important at the end of life. Tell yourself that it's just stuff.
- Consider whether some items could bless someone else.
- Talk to God; ask for help to remember that your life is a mere breath in comparison to eternity.
- Cherish the people in your life; take more time to visit with loved ones and friends, keeping your heart focused on what's important.

six-month slide

About six months after Austin died, the entire Erickson family (minus kids) went to an all-inclusive resort in Mexico to celebrate my in-laws' fiftieth wedding anniversary. (More on this later.) While walking on the beach one day, I felt so heavy, like the sand was filling my legs and pulling my heart deep underwater. I just plopped down right in the sand and sobbed. I didn't care if anyone saw me (for once), and I just let out the ugly cry.

As the sobbing subsided, I tried to take deep breaths and let the ocean rhythm steady me. But then I started crying out to God. If I'm honest, it was more like shouting inside my heart. It went something like this:

"How can this be happening? I don't want to celebrate *our* fiftieth wedding anniversary so many years from now without Austin! Ethan will be an only child. How could You do this?! It's too much. This will keep drowning me!

"This is NEVER going to be okay! I hate this!"

Welcome to the six-month slide.

The six-month slide back into the deep and dark pit of grief is likely to happen. I've spoken with enough grieving people to know that our experience was not unique. Around six months, this thing you're going through becomes *more* real.

I know what you're thinking: "You're kidding, right?" Nope. I wish the grief journey didn't keep circling, circling. Like a shark circling its prey, so is the grief pit, waiting for you to lose your footing and slide back down into the dark hole.

I hope you are reading this before the ground starts to slide under your feet and you wonder what is happening. I thought my mind was really cracking up this time. I didn't feel like missing Austin every single day was getting any easier. It was getting *more* difficult. I thought, "What is happening to me?"

It's tough to tell people (who are expecting you to keep getting better) that you are sliding backwards in your grief. It feels like you couldn't possibly explain what is happening to you. Your heart feels heavier every day, and the replay is back with a vengeance. You can't tell anyone about this horrific turn of events. Everyone is so worried about you already. It doesn't feel safe to disclose that you are doing *worse* now than during the funeral.

Oh friend, I wish I could lift this from you and give you a big, long hug and tell you it's going to be okay. Now you're saying: "It's not going to be okay. It's *never* going to be okay!" I used to hate it when people would say it was going to be okay. It didn't feel true. But, I'm writing now to tell you, ten years later, it *can* be true. If you keep your eyes on heaven and keep your heart searching for God, you can fight against this never-ending darkness. You must keep fighting. There really is no other choice.

I know you feel tired. I know you are unbearably sad. I remember. Sometimes, I'm back there. A week or two, even a month, can creep in and yank me back down into the pit. I know that's not what you want to hear. I know this might be difficult to read, but I promised to tell you the truth. The truth is this: your grief is likely to get more exhausting before it gets better.

It is also true that it *will* get better as time passes. Just don't get caught unawares if, out of the blue and for no apparent reason, you have a bad day, a rough week, a dark and lonely month. Those times will get shorter and shorter,

I'm not saying that life will ever be okay without your child. I am saying that you will be okay—eventually.

less and less frequent, as life rolls on. That's why I say that it will be okay. I'm not saying life will ever be okay without your child. I am only saying that *you* will be okay—eventually. Your life will hit more of an even keel. The dips and valleys will smooth out.

But it won't happen without God.

Nevertheless, in your great mercies you did not make an end of them or forsake them, for you are a gracious and merciful God.

Now, therefore, our God, the great, the mighty,
and the awesome God, who keeps covenant
and steadfast love, let not all the hardship
seem little to you.
(NEHEMIAH 9:31–32)

Back on the beach, I reached around in the sand and picked up a nearby shell. I threw it as hard as I could. I saw another shell and picked it up, but this time I studied it. It was thick and had deep, rough ridges. I looked out at the waves. I was ready to talk to God now:

"I feel like I'm never going to get my feet under me. Losing Austin feels like these ocean waves. Gut-wrenching pain keeps hitting me, just like these waves, over and over and over again. Never-ending, always hammering the sand, hammering me. Even if I do get my feet under me, the grief wave comes too soon again and knocks me back down. Just as I think I am getting up, BAM, another wave of grief."

My breath was coming heavy now. Panic was rising. Like the waves, I felt my mind about to crash . . . again. "It's too much. I'm never going to survive this. It's just going to keep coming, just like this ocean. I can't do this. I can't."

It came next like a whisper into my mind, deep inside my soul: "Pick up this shell . . . on your left." On my left side, I saw another shell. It had the same shape and color as the thick, ridged one in my right hand. The shell I picked up with my left hand, however, was feather light. It was thin and smooth. No rough edges. The waves had smoothed this shell into something beautiful.

A small, still voice spoke healing into my soul, something like this:

"Your grief will be like these shells. Right now it is heavy, rough, with deep and painful grooves. But, someday, it will smooth out. You will always carry it, like a shell tucked into your pocket, but your grief will be like this lighter shell. Your grief will become easier, smoother, less painful. Just like these ocean waves worked the shell from the rough, heavy shell down into the thin, smooth one, your pain will be the same. It *will* work its way down to something smaller, less painful. Yes, it will remain, but it won't always be so heavy and hard."

I just stared at the two shells, one in each hand. I was nodding my head in silent understanding as tears continued to roll down my face.

"Thank you, God," I whispered into the waves. "Thank you, Father."

Calling Out for Rescue

I don't tell a lot of people about these moments I've had with God. Those moments when my heart is broken and I think that I cannot hold up under the weight of this grief, and I cry out to God. I ask Him for help. I ask Him to heal my hurt, to put some heavenly balm over the throbbing wound in my soul.

Our loving God has responded almost always, in a

hundred different ways. Some as simple as suddenly being able to catch my breath. You know how sometimes the pain is so great, it feels physical, like a tight pressure around your chest? I ask for heavenly help when that tightness settles over me. Sometimes, I simply feel the hurt being lifted from me, like someone just lifted a sack of potatoes or a heavy backpack off my shoulders. Other times have been bigger, bolder moments like the seashells on the beach in Mexico.

None of these moments involved hearing God's audible voice. I'm certain I couldn't hold up under His mighty breath! These are Holy Spirit moments, deep inside my heart and mind. Jesus promised if you put your faith in Him, He would send the Helper, the Spirit of Truth, the Counselor, to be with you forever. The Holy Spirit is an earthly promise to every single believer in Jesus Christ as Son of the living God, Lord, and Savior (John 14–16).

I've given up trying to wrap my logical mind around it. I simply cannot make sense of the actual presence of God in my daily life. The more I sought God, read my Bible, prayed, cried out to Him, the more I felt the Holy Spirit—the more overwhelmed I became by the loving care of our Creator. He will never leave me or forsake me (Josh. 1:5). No matter how many times I slide back into the pit, God stands ready to rescue me.

God stands ready to rescue you as well. It may not feel like it. I definitely recall days when I could not feel or "see" God at all. But I kept talking to Him, crying out to Him, all the same. I think it was my relentless pursuit of God during my darkest hours of grief that allowed the Holy Spirit to lift my chin, to give me relief, to let me feel God's comfort. Please, don't stop talking to God. Don't stop seeking God's face when the darkness settles in. It is during your darkest hours that you need the shining light of God's presence the most.

When the six-month slide opens its treacherous jaws and pulls at you to slide easily into the pit of grief, fight back. Cry out to God. Demand that He fulfill His promises to you. Now, I know some of you might have gasped at what I just told you to do. Demand something from almighty God?! Who does she think she is? Didn't Job get in trouble for that?

Here's what I mean: usually people don't "demand" something unless they think they're entitled to it. If you sit there in your tears and think you're not worthy of God's help, then you're thinking too small about our mighty God. I say demand because I mean "stand firm" on the promises of God. People say that a lot. Stand firm on the promises of God. Stand firm in your faith, and so on. I mean the same thing, but when I talk to God like my Father God, it tends to sound more like a demand: "*You said* that You would never leave me or forsake me. So why can't I feel You? If You've never left my side, then allow me to see You, to feel You, right now. At this very moment, I need to feel You with me *right now.*"

I think God is okay with me crying out to Him about the things He has promised His children, all those who believe in Jesus as Lord and Savior. I get the right to be called a child of God. After submitting to Jesus, I get the right to be called a daughter of the King of kings.

I admit—I am a straightforward and direct person, so my

prayers tend to sound a bit more like demands. Never losing respect or reverence for the almighty God but also not standing far off from Him, hoping He might glance my way. I trot boldly up to Him and make my requests known to Him, which is why Philippians 4:4–8 are my "life verses." These verses say when we approach God with thanksgiving and make our requests known to Him, a peace beyond our comprehension will guard our hearts and our minds in Christ Jesus.

This faith that God calls me daughter and hears my prayers is steadfast because whenever I pray the promises God makes in the Bible, I always feel differently when I'm finished praying. I do not always get what I ask for, but somehow my heart and mind *feel* different than before I started. You can think it's wishful thinking or just venting feelings if you'd like, but something that feels much "bigger" and more secure washes over me when I pray, especially if I pray the promises I read in my Bible. You should try it for yourself and see what happens!

Let's look at my life verses and how I pray those verses as promises that God made directly to me. Philippians 4:4–8 (NASB) states:

Rejoice in the Lord always; again I will say, rejoice!
Let your gentle spirit be known to all men. The Lord is
near. Be anxious for nothing, but in everything
by prayer and supplication with thanksgiving let your
requests be made known to God. And the peace of God,
which surpasses all comprehension, will guard
your hearts and your minds in Christ Jesus.

Finally, brethren, whatever is true, whatever is honorable,
whatever is right, whatever is pure,
whatever is lovely, whatever is of good repute, if there
is any excellence and if anything worthy of praise,
dwell on these things.

When I pray these verses, it goes something like this:

"God, I am trying to rejoice in You, but it is hard today. Help me to praise You. I'm angry and tired today, but Lord, give me that gentle spirit. God, You promised that You are near, so let me feel or see Your presence right now. I need You here with me. My worries and anxiety are high right now, God, so please help me be anxious for nothing. I'm so grateful for all of my blessings, O Lord. Please hear my prayers. (Next, I pray about the things that are worrying me or causing me anxiety.) God, You promised that Your peace would fill me up after I pray to You. Please give me Your peace and let it be beyond my comprehension.

"Father, guard my heart and my mind in the power of Jesus. Lord, let my heart and mind shift to the things that are good in my life. Let only those things that are true, right, excellent, praiseworthy, pure, honorable, and lovely run through my mind today. In the powerful name of Jesus I pray. Amen" (which means "let it be so"!).

Finally, as you fight the six-month slide back into the dark parts of losing your child, may I encourage you to try just one verse as a promise prayer. Memorize this verse and ask that God come through on His promise:

The LORD is near to the brokenhearted
and saves the crushed in spirit.
(PSALM 34:18)

SURVIVAL STEP:
Beware the Six-Month Slide . . . and Fight It!

Ideas:

- You are not losing your mind. The six-month slide is real and is just the cycle of grief that will circle in and out of you for a while. Get a journal and write about this next season.
- Consider joining a grief group. Shared experiences can strengthen us. Use Google to find a grief group near you and to experience that you are not alone.
- Remember your "let it out" and "stop the replay" techniques; you'll need them again.
- Go ahead and tell a trusted friend that grief is smacking you around right now but that you intend to fight back.

Ask your friend to send you a text each day for the next week to encourage you; then, pick another friend and repeat until you feel better.

- Find some Bible verses that speak to what you are feeling right now. Write them down; memorize them, if you can.
- Find some Bible verses that make promises—the ones that make you say, "I wish that were true for me, but I don't feel that way." Write them down and start "demanding" those promises to feel true for you right now.

SPIRITUAL STEP:
Start Praying the Promises in the Bible

I am certain that God's Word saved me from the pit of grief. I am also certain that it would have made no sense to me if I didn't know Jesus was my Savior and had I not asked the Helper, the Holy Spirit, to teach me all things (John 14:26). Each day before I started reading my Bible, I would ask God to help me make sense of it. I would ask God to speak to me through it. I requested healing as my tears dripped over the words.

It is because of the many times God revealed something with powerful healing words or thoughts that I beg you to pick up a Bible and read it each morning. I know without hesitation that God will speak to you through His Word, if you are willing to hear it.

Ideas:

Instead of listing several ideas here, I'd like to give you just one task to complete. A kind of "try it and see" request. Try the steps below and listen for the whisper of God in your soul:

- Ask God to reveal Himself to you through this exercise. Tell God you need Him, that you want Him in your life.
- Read Psalm 143 in your Bible or even online.
- Read Psalm 143 again, but this time say it out loud and change the words as follows:
    "the enemy" = "this grief"
    "my enemies" = "my grief" and
    "destroy all those *who* afflict my soul" = "destroy all those *thoughts that* afflict my soul"
- Write Psalm 143 on a piece of paper with these word changes.
- Pray or "demand" these promises each morning before you start your day. Claim the promises as a child of God, entitled to the things the King of kings has said He will give to you.

let Him have it!

About six years after Austin died, my brother Mark was diagnosed with terminal brain cancer. His tumor was the most
aggressive kind of cancer. Our family was devastated. Again?
Really, God? My brother Jeff died in a car accident in 1989. We
lost Austin to something as common as strep throat in 2008.
Now we must face death in our immediately family once again?

In addition to immediate family, Devin and I lost several
people so close to us. One of Devin's best friends died from
cancer about six months after Austin died. Miss Alma, our
nanny (whom we called our boys' Arizona grandma), died
from breast cancer just two years after Austin went to heaven.
My legal assistant and right hand of seven years died from
cancer about four years after Austin.

Now, my brother Mark? You've got to be kidding me.

My brother fought hard, and many people prayed hard.
After surgery, radiation, and chemo, Mark and his family had
a brief respite from the cancer. But it came back with a vengeance about a year later. I remember having a conversation

with my mom after we found out that Mark's tumor returned in a very aggressive way.

"God and I are going to have a serious talk about this," I said to Mom.

"I just don't understand," she murmured with her head hung low in sorrow.

"Oh, believe me"—I raised my voice in anger—"He's going to hear it from me! I'm going to let Him have it! This is completely unfair, and He knows it. This is unbearable and too much."

My mom looked at me, wide-eyed. "I don't think you should talk to God like that, do you?" she asked.

"Yes, I do. I do, Mom, because He's my Father in heaven. He's the Almighty, all-powerful God. He can take it!"

I kept ranting. But as I did, something inside me softened. And I realized that I had developed something priceless and precious: a *relationship* with God Himself.

I needed my mom to understand my relationship with God. So I said, "Mom, I talk to God every day. I believe He talks to me as well, through my Bible and the Holy Spirit. He knows me . . . and my temper. He loves me more than I can imagine. Just like when Austin would pitch a fit, I still loved him no matter what. Our God loves us like that. No matter what. Even when we pitch a fit," I told her as I hugged her tight.

She looked a bit skeptical and still worried about me when we parted, but I felt like a thousand pounds had been lifted off my back. It was true. I really could vent, rage, and stomp my feet like a child, and God would still love me just the same. He really would patiently wait, like millions of parents every day, until I stopped my temper tantrum.

From that day, my conversations with God grew even deeper. I knew I could trust Him with my innermost dreadful thoughts and feelings. On some level, I had come to understand that God knows my thoughts and feelings before I even dare to speak them to Him. So, my expression of them is no surprise to Him. What God desires from us is a relationship, a deep and personal one.

> Holding back what is truly on your heart and in your mind is a death sentence in any relationship, even one with your Almighty Father.

You can't develop a relationship through a filter. Holding back what is truly on your heart and in your mind is a death sentence in any relationship, even one with your Almighty Father. The One who loves you more than you can imagine stands ready to take whatever you need to dish out!

I know some of you might be cringing right now, wondering how I can act with such disrespect toward God. Please do not misunderstand me. I do believe we need to keep God in reverence and understand His holiness and His power. We need to stand always in awe of Him. We must understand that He alone is God. Of course.

God Understands!

What I am saying here is that God *understands* this kind of pain. God lost His one (and only) Son to torture and murder. God was forced to turn His mighty back on His only Son so that our sins could be forgiven. God allowed His only Son to die a criminal's death. You know how you very quickly connect with someone who has also lost a child? When you look into the eyes of that other parent who has also faced the horror of losing a child, there is an instant *knowing* that takes place between you. An immediate and unspoken bond passes between you, as only another grieving parent could understand. For a moment, both of you feel less lonely, more understood. Likely, if given time, you would speak openly about the dark feelings you've experienced in grief, sharing feelings you wouldn't dare tell someone else. Only another parent who has lost a child could understand.

That other parent who has lost a child *is* God. He is looking at you with eyes that express the unspeakable bond among those grieving a child. God gets it. It is with this deep bond that I feel free to sling my utmost horrifying thoughts at Him. It is because I feel completely safe with Him, as I would a fellow grieving parent, that I can abandon the bounds of social decency. No filter needed between me and my God. He gets it. He can take it. He loves me. He knows this pain. It is from this place in my heart that I believe I can pitch a fit with God, never from a place of disrespect or lack of reverence.

In addition, as He walked this earth, Jesus showed us the

feelings of God with regard to death and grieving. Jesus faced sickness, pain, and death during His time here. And John, His beloved disciple, tells us in his Gospel that Jesus wept. When faced with the grief expressed by those around Him, when considering their heartbreak, Jesus wept.

Jesus wept. It cannot be overstated or repeated often enough. Jesus did not chide his friends for weeping. Jesus did not reprimand Mary or Martha for expressing their heartfelt cries. The questions like, "Why did you allow this to happen?" or "Where were you when we needed you?" were not met with a rebuke from Jesus. His responses were twofold.

First, He asked, "Do you believe I am the Christ?" In other words, He wanted them to stand firm in their faith during this time of sorrow and rest in the hope of heaven, secure in salvation through Him. Specifically, Jesus said, "I am the resurrection and the life; he who believes in Me will live even if he dies, and everyone who lives and believes in Me will never die. Do you believe this?" (John 11:25–26 NASB).

Even knowing the answer to this question, and even knowing that He was about to raise Lazarus from the dead, Jesus wept. After reminding the women of their faith, Jesus wept. He was moved by the grief of people. He felt the pain. Otherwise, He wouldn't have cried. The apostle John wrote that Jesus was deeply moved by the mourners (John 11:11–45). Jesus is deeply moved by our pain. He will cry along with us. It is with these assurances that I allow myself to fall at His feet and cry out, shouting all that is in my heart, knowing that He will weep with me.

If you are so angry at God that you don't even want to think about speaking to Him right now, I understand that feeling, too. He built us with the emotion of anger, so He understands that emotion as well. Even Jesus expressed anger sometimes. But isn't it true that anger withheld, anger pushed down deep and never expressed, becomes a giant pus-filled wound? We don't need this wound of losing a child to get any bigger, do we?

You may have heard this marriage advice: never go to bed angry. The idea of never letting the sun go down while you are still holding on to your anger comes from this verse:

Therefore, having put away falsehood, let each one of you speak the truth with his neighbor, for we are members one of another. Be angry and do not sin; do not let the sun go down on your anger, and give no opportunity to the devil.
(EPHESIANS 4:25-27)

I think the same applies to our relationship with God. Express your anger and try your best to let it go. Do not give the devil, your enemy, any chance to separate you from God. When you are down and injured, bleeding directly from your heart, the enemy of your soul would love to have your grief wound be filled with anger, seething and withheld, so that you stay mad at God. If your anger allows you to stay turned away from God, then the devil can have his way with you and your life will, in fact, remain miserable.

If you express your anger and lay it at God's feet (or fling it in His face, where He will allow it to fall at the foot of the cross), then God can whisper into your soul, He can gather you in His arms and rock you until the hurt subsides a bit. Let God have your fury. Let the fullness of your fury loose so that it does not remain as a tool to turn you away from God. Let loose your anguish and find that God remains, standing faithful and true, to say "I love you, daughter. I'm so sorry this hurts so much." Let God have it all, and let His tears heal your soul.

SURVIVAL STEP:
Let Out ALL of Your Emotions

Set up some time *today* to get away from everyone and everything. Allow God to have the full measure of your heart and all the emotions that go with it. I pray that you will allow yourself to tangibly feel the heart of God weeping with you.

Ideas:

- Stay home for the day. Call in sick to work or get someone to cover any other daily needs, and spend the day expressing every single emotion swimming inside you.
- Journal each emotion that comes to mind as you allow yourself to feel the loss of your child.
- Say all the awful things out loud, and ask God to take those thoughts away from you.

- Ask God if He really loves you, and keep an open mind for something to happen to show you His love.
- Break more dishes! (see "Let It Out Ideas" on pages 64–65).
- Consider joining Grief Share or some other support group so you can learn that you are not alone in your questions or emotions.
- Write down all the questions you would ask God if He were sitting at your kitchen table.
- Read Psalm 69 (use www.Biblegateway.com if you don't have a Bible yet; then email me and I'll send a Bible to you free of charge). See how David (you know this one, think David and Goliath) cried out his pain. God called David "a man after my heart." The Lord loved David deeply, but David suffered and sinned, just like us. David was close enough to God to express his feelings and cry out to God to answer—to answer quickly!

SPIRITUAL STEP:
Be Honest with God

A Christian life is very simply a genuine, heartfelt relationship with God. If all the trappings of "religion" or "church" were stripped away, the heart of every person would still desire to know God. Humans were made in the image of God, and we were designed to interact with Him. Religion and church can be beautiful places where we connect and grow with other believers. The local church and a body of believers coming together is so important and definitely is part of a healthy Christian's life. The most essential and initial component, however, is your relationship with God.

If you've accepted Jesus as Savior and Lord, then a relationship with God is *possible*. It's up to you how vibrant and close you want it to be. Just like in any human relationship, communication is key. Open, honest communication is the cornerstone of every great relationship. The same applies to your relationship with God. If you don't spend time talking to Him, or if you filter what you say to Him, then your relationship might be too shallow to help you through the valley of death. The valley of grief is deep and dark. You'll need to have a lot of conversations with God to find your way through it and come out on the other side. True, your life will never look or feel the same without your child, but you can find joy, happiness, and contentment again. You can and you will *if* you cry out to God.

> If all the trappings of "religion" or "church" were stripped away, the heart of every person would still desire to know God.

Try reading the first half of the Psalms in the Bible. You will hear how often God's people cried out for help. Psalm 69 is a picture of David's raw emotions. Yet, before David closes the psalm, he turns back to praising God and remembering that God hears the needy. In the last line of Psalm 69, David reminds himself and others, "The descendants of His servants will inherit [God's kingdom], and those who love His name will dwell in it" (Ps. 69:36 NASB).

Someday, those who believe in Jesus Christ as their Savior will dwell in perfect peace in heaven. As you cry out to God, try to end by circling back to God's promise to you: eternal life in heaven. Eventually, God *will* fix your broken heart. In the meantime, it's okay to cry out to Him as often and as broken as you need to. In the book of Job, we are reminded of this special privilege:

> *But I would speak to the Almighty, and I desire to argue*
> *my case with God. . . . Though he slay me,*
> *I will hope in him; yet I will argue my ways to his face.*
> *This will be my salvation, that the godless*
> *shall not come before him.*
> (JOB 13:3, 15–16)

Ideas:

- If you don't normally talk out loud to God, try it for two weeks.
- Journal your heart's cry to God.
- Read Psalms 69 and 107 (and lots of others, especially in the first half of the Psalms).
- Skim through the book of Job, and pay attention when Job is talking. See how many emotions you can find in

Job's conversations with others; you will see that Job was honest about his feelings and how he wanted to question God about all that happened to him.

- Read *A Grief Observed* by C. S. Lewis (which he wrote after his wife died).
- Read *The Pursuit of God* by A.W. Tozer.
- Read *A Sacred Sorrow* by Michael Card (a book on grieving as shown through the lives of Job, Jeremiah, David, and Jesus).
- Read *A Grace Disguised* by Jerry L. Sittser (written after he lost his wife, mother, and young daughter in the same car accident).

Chapter 8

holidays, anniversaries, and birthdays

The days we gather with family and celebrate are, of course, some of the most difficult days to tackle on this grief journey. The gaping hole left by our missing child looms large as holidays or birthdays approach. The celebration can be several weeks in the future, but our hearts can feel the despair that threatens to overtake us, even now. The anniversary of your child's death or burial threaten as you flip the calendar to the month before *that* month. Those specific dates on the calendar cause us to want to turn back time and go back to the way it was before we lost our child. Like Job in the verse above, we yearn for the days when our family was complete, especially during certain seasons and dates throughout the year.

I can dread April starting around Thanksgiving. Once

Thanksgiving begins to pop up in stores, I immediately dread going through another holiday season without Austin. So, that lump in my throat and the spinning rewind of my mind begin in November, runs through the holidays, and keeps on until late January and early February when Ethan and Devin have their birthdays. Before I can get a handle on myself and my sadness, March arrives and signals my birthday, which is only two weeks from Austin's birthday and a month before his passing date, both in April.

Next, you have May and Mother's Day, followed by June and Father's Day. It seems by the time my husband and I can take a breath without effort, it's July. So we have July, August, September, and October to recharge before the cycle begins again. Anyone else?

> I can dread April starting around Thanksgiving.

As the cycle repeats itself each year, some things do get easier, I promise you. You *will* find ways to handle the anticipation, the actual day(s), and the recovery period. How you will do that depends on when your dates fall and what the circumstances surrounding your child's death came to pass. What I can recommend is a repeat of the notion that this is your loss and yours alone. So, you need to do what comforts you without worrying about what others (except the other parent(s) and siblings) may think.

I am extremely blessed that my husband and I tend to desire the same thing when it comes to these difficult days:

for the day to pass and quickly, with as little pain as possible. We don't do anything special during holidays to recognize Austin. We don't celebrate his birthday. We don't mark the day he passed in any certain way, other than spending the day together and experiencing some extra-tight hugs. Since Austin was buried on the family farm, we don't have a habit of visiting his grave on certain days. It may sound odd to some of you, but we literally do not call attention to the gaping "Austin-hole" in our family, ever. We feel it every single day, so these other days we just want to pass more quickly than usual.

Since this works for both Devin and me, this is what we do—nothing. And that works for us. We don't give a rip what others might want to do. If they want to do something on their own, we leave those personal moments to them. I hope this gives you permission to stop doing things if you sincerely don't want to participate in outward memorials of your child. It's okay. It's your choice, and no one has to get it but you. You might need to communicate your feelings if others are involved, but that is the end of your responsibility, in my humble opinion.

If you are lucky, the people in your life will be aware of the mounting tension and give you a little extra tender loving care as difficult days approach. Most often, I have found, the days before and the days after a holiday or anniversary/birthday are more difficult than the actual day.

It's as if the anticipation of an upcoming important date, and then the recovery after that day, are more intense than the pain inflicted on the actual date we dread. My theory is that those people in our lives who are supporting and tending to us during these times mostly reach out to us on the actual day, which is great. Telephone calls, emails, texts, posts, etc., all make us feel like our child is remembered and that we are loved.

That being said, in those early years, I would often blast out a text or email a day or two before and let people know that I did not intend to respond for a few days and that I hoped they didn't take it personally. I just knew I needed some space and slack during those hard days, so I tried to let people know ahead of time how much I appreciated their sweet thoughts. Many years later, the volume of calls, texts, emails, and posts has dropped so drastically, I don't feel overwhelmed by them anymore.

You may have noticed this reduction if you are a few years into your grief journey. It seems that people remember for a year or two, and then it drops way down. And that's okay, too. Try your best to have understanding for those who have stopped reaching out on the important days. It's not that they have forgotten your child, it's just that the date doesn't stick out in their minds like it does in your mind and heart. It's not that they love you any less or support you any less, it's only that you are doing so well they don't think or see that you need their words of encouragement now.

It is this falloff that leads me to remind you that this is your loss and yours alone. You are the only one who will be held hostage by so many days on the calendar. Time will pass and wounds will heal for others who experienced loss when your child died, but yours will remain as long as you continue to turn that calendar from month to month. So, my friend, take care of you. Do what brings *you* comfort on the difficult days.

If it would bring you comfort to throw a huge party for your child's birthday every year, then do it! If you would feel peace each year as you hang his stocking on the fireplace along with your other children's, do it. If her favorite holiday was Valentine's Day and you buy roses and candy to honor her, that is great. You get to do whatever you want on those tough days.

SURVIVAL STEP:
Do What YOU Need to Do

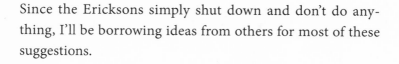

Since the Ericksons simply shut down and don't do anything, I'll be borrowing ideas from others for most of these suggestions.

Ideas:

- Invite a friend over or make plans with someone. Let them know what day it is for you.
- Make plans to do something different, unusual, fun.
- Let friends know that the days before and the day after might be tough, too.
- Make a list of the rough days, and make sure your support people have them in their calendars. It's okay to ask for help and to help them remember.
- Release balloons.

- Decorate at the cemetery or burial site.
- Bake a cake and celebrate.
- Write a tribute about your child each year.
- Journal your dreams for your child; write your wishes for her life.
- Create scrapbooks of your favorite pictures, and group by holiday and different birthdays.
- Make a playlist of music to soothe your soul.
- Ask your church to pray for you; get on several prayer lists around your dreaded days.
- Do something indulgent, like schedule a massage, send yourself flowers, get a manicure/pedicure, or spend a movie marathon day at the theatre.
- Settle in with your pajamas, Netflix, popcorn, and ice cream; draw the blinds, turn your phone off, and just relax (this is my contribution!).

SPIRITUAL STEP:
Set Out Reminders

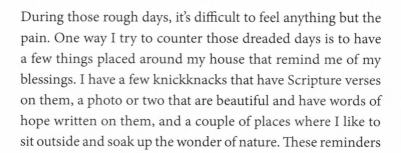

During those rough days, it's difficult to feel anything but the pain. One way I try to counter those dreaded days is to have a few things placed around my house that remind me of my blessings. I have a few knickknacks that have Scripture verses on them, a photo or two that are beautiful and have words of hope written on them, and a couple of places where I like to sit outside and soak up the wonder of nature. These reminders are necessary for me. Without these reminders of God, I might slip back into bitterness.

God knows this about me, about us. After God led His people out of Egypt by sending seven plagues on the Egyptians and then splitting the Red Sea so that the Jewish people walked through it on dry ground, those very same people seemed to forget what God did for them (right in front of their own eyes!). The people began to complain as they traveled through the desert to the land God had promised them. Uh-oh. Not a great idea. God was a bit ticked off that they had forgotten how amazing He was to them just a short time before. Their grumbling resulted in God's disciplining them as a loving father would his children, and the Jewish people had to wait forty years before they would finally get to inhabit the land promised. God essentially put them into time-out for their disrespect.

When their time-out was completed, God told their new leader, Joshua, that He was about to bring the people into the promised land. There was one problem. The people would have to cross the Jordan River, which was at its highest flood stage. No worries, God explained to Joshua. He planned to show Himself to the Jewish people *again* by allowing them to cross the Jordan on dry ground. God said He would stop the water flow as soon as the leaders stepped into the water.

I can just see God up there shaking His head and thinking, "They better not forget this again!" I also think this new plan showed how God intended to partner with the Jewish people during this next season. He would be working *with* them, but they would have to do their part by taking the first obedient step. As God always does, He did what He said He would do: as soon as the leaders stepped into the Jordan carrying the ark of the covenant (holding the Ten Commandments and symbolic of the presence of God), the Jordan river split, and nearly a million people were able to walk through it on dry ground!

Next, God told Joshua this:

"Take twelve men from the people, from each tribe a man, and command them, saying, 'Take twelve stones from here out of the midst of the Jordan, from the very place where the priests' feet stood firmly, and bring them over with you and lay them down in the place where you lodge tonight.'"

(JOSHUA 4:2–3)

Joshua did just that and told the Jewish people:

"Take up each of you a stone upon his shoulder, according to the number of the tribes of the people of Israel, that this may be a sign among you. When your children ask in time to come, 'What do those stones mean to you?' then you shall tell them that the waters of the Jordan were cut off before the ark of the covenant of the LORD. *When it passed over the Jordan, the waters of the Jordan were cut off. So these stones shall be to the people of Israel a memorial forever."*

(JOSHUA 4:5–7)

You see, God knew about our human nature. He knew that when times got tough, and those times would come, we tend to forget all the good things in our lives. When trouble hits, we tend to throw a giant pity party. We really like the good stuff from God, but when something breaks our hearts and seems impossible to handle, all those blessings fade into the background. We need reminders.

God had the Jewish people use twelve stones to create a memorial to the moment when He did something miraculous for them. I like to think that if I ever experienced a miracle like that in person, I'd never stop talking about it. My grandchildren's grandchildren would tell the story generations later because I'd never shut up about it. I'd never lose my sense of awe at what God did for me.

Yet I know this isn't true. I've already forgotten some things God did for me. I never even *knew* about many other things I'm sure He did for me through people and circumstances. Especially on those difficult days, I tend to forget the multitude of amazing things God does for me every day. I need those memorial stones!

Today, look around at your surroundings. Do you have a place to live? A car? Food to eat? Clothing? Clean water? The list could go on and on. All things exist because of God. Create a list of the tangible things you have that are a blessing to you. Next, create a list of some of the good things that have happened to you over the years. You had a child. Some people never get to experience a child in their life. Do you have a job or an income? Did you have a loving family? Was school easy or fun for you? Have you ever seen the ocean? Taken a trip? Have you ever felt like God must have been watching over you in a certain moment in time?

All these things are stones. These normal things of life are our memorial rocks. Gather them. Stack them up. Create a memorial of all the things that are "good" in your life. Somehow, create something that will remind you that you are, in fact, surrounded by good (even though it doesn't feel like it many days throughout the year).

Ideas:

- Choose your most difficult month. Each day that month, read one chapter of the book of Joshua in the Bible (there are twenty-four chapters, so you have a bit of wiggle room).
- Make the lists I mentioned above—one for the tangible good things and another for the intangible good memories. Keep those lists handy for the bad days.
- Create or buy something that reminds you of all the good things God has allowed in your life.
- Ask someone to send you a text reminder of something good in your life, even now that you are forced to live it without your child.
- Make a list of all the good things that happened to your child while you were blessed to have him/her.
- Read the Psalms, and notice how most psalms always

end by praising God for who He is and/or what He has done or will do in the future.

- Make a playlist of music that praises God. Even if you can't muster up the feelings, let the music praise God for you, over you.

ordinary days: what to do about the triggers

Perhaps before you lost a child, you thought that it would be the holidays, anniversaries, and birthdays that would be among the most difficult days. But, now that you are on the other side of this terrifying loss, you realize this untenable truth: it is the everyday life you fear most. The ordinary days leave you feeling most alone. Each morning you arise feeling tired already. Everyday life has a gaping hole that looms larger than you could ever imagine or ever think to survive. Yet, survive it we must. We remain on this planet for some reason, even if we cannot see the point right now.

Since there are too many ways, times, and places we miss our child each day, this chapter cannot hold all that we need to tend to our broken hearts. What I hope to pass on in this chapter are some ideas for what I believe to be the most common triggers of intense pain during an ordinary day. My prayer is to give your weary soul a bit of rest in some practical ways, but the true rest you need can only be found in God and our Lord Jesus. My relationship with God is the only way I have a chance of surviving the everyday hole in my life from losing Austin.

If you have any questions about God, Jesus, heaven, or anything else in this book, please do not hesitate to reach out to me through my website at KimAErickson.com. I'll answer your questions honestly and to the best of my mama-ability!

Jesus said:

"Come to me, all who labor and are heavy laden,
and I will give you rest. Take my yoke upon you,
and learn from me, for I am gentle and lowly in heart,
and you will find rest for your souls."
(MATTHEW 11:28–29)

Below are several "Survival Steps" to help you through those "ordinary" days.

"The Question": How Many Kids Do You Have?

Unless you are very early on in this grief journey, I'm certain you have faced this question. This question causes you to pause, and the other person looks at you confused, wondering why you have to think about how many children you have! The question comes from a well-meaning new acquaintance or maybe even just some unsuspecting person at a park, library, or grocery store. They don't mean to send you for a griefspin, but it happens nonetheless.

If I say that I have two children, then the next questions are going to be boys/girls and how old? Well, shoot, now how do I answer the how old question? Ugh. It's just easier to say one and then, "Yes, he's my only," and face the judgment that sometimes comes from mothers who have multiple children. The speculation I see on their faces when I say I only have one child is infinitely better than the horror on their face if I tell them about Austin . . . in the park, or at the store, or in the library. It's like dropping a bomb in the middle of a sunny day. I do not like it.

For a while, when someone asked how many children I have, I would say (quite cleverly if I do say so myself), "I have a three-year-old boy *at home*. His name is Ethan and he's the sweetest thing." I tried my best to deflect the question and shift focus to Ethan. Too many times, however, the person was listening closely and dared to ask follow-up questions. Do you have an older child, one who's left the house already, like in college? Do you have other kids from a previous marriage, who are living with their dad? Then, I'd have to drop the bomb. "No, we lost our three-year-old son to strep throat last year . . ." Now that good listener is crying. Not a good thing when someone is just making small talk. Again, ugh.

Since my little trick didn't work too often, and the truth was just too difficult to say in polite conversation, I usually said that I just had one child. Until, that is, Ethan began to talk. If Ethan heard the question, he would usually answer, "I have a brother, but he died and he's waiting for us in heaven." As he'd run off to play or grab something from the shelf, the poor unsuspecting person couldn't believe her ears or that a toddler just told her that he had a dead brother. Dare I say it again? UGH.

But what's a mom to do? My heart cried each time I said that I only have one boy. It's not true. In my heart and forever, I have two boys. Two rowdy, silly, active, smart, athletic boys. After ten years, my heart still thinks I have these two boys, Austin and Ethan, who are so much like their Daddy.

So, do you want the good news? After all these years, I have *finally* landed on what I am comfortable saying about my biggest heartbreak to virtual strangers. When someone asks me how many kids I have, I say, "I have two boys, one in heaven and one at home."

Usually this answer is gentle enough to avoid the bomb of a child dying and "closed" enough that I don't have to answer a bunch of personal and very difficult questions for a stranger. If a friendship grows out of this initial conversation, then it is comfortable to share the heartache and details of losing Austin some other time. I pray my experience and struggle helps you avoid some of the really tough and awkward ordinary life moments!

Adult Child Loss?

Since I have lost two adult brothers and two adult first cousins, I can tell you that my mom and my aunt have no problem answering this question. The question does not cause them to pause or stumble. It may cause them pain in remembrance, but it is not a struggle to find the "right" answer. My mom always says she has five children, without hesitation. She was surprised the "how many kids do you have" question was difficult for me to answer. In her mind, the answer is always the same. My Aunt Katie answers the same way as my mom. She always says she has nine kids. My theory is that losing an adult child might not lead to the follow-up questions that seemed to take place when I lost a toddler and had a baby following my footsteps. Also, another theory, my mom and aunt live in very small, rural communities where everyone knows everyone else. It's not very often that they engage in conversation with others who do not know them and their family history/story.

Miscarriage or Stillbirth

Unfortunately, our culture doesn't seem to recognize miscarriages or stillbirths the same as the loss of a child who lives out some days on this earth. If you, like me, have suffered one or more of these losses, please know I think many of the things I have written in this book apply to you and those losses as well. Having suffered a miscarriage, infertility issues, another miscarriage, and finally the fact of not being able to have more children, I know firsthand that these losses are real, painful, and also never-ending. The losses of two babies to early miscarriage also make me long for heaven when I will finally get to meet them! I cannot wait. Ethan thinks they will be two sisters. We'll see. Someday, my friend, we'll see them, whole and beautiful and perfect.

Also, a great resource is a book by John MacArthur: *Safe in the Arms of God*. I highly recommend it for why we can *know* that our babies are in heaven!

The Regular Places

These are the places that are common to your everyday life: grocery store, Walmart, gas station, Target, the mall, restaurants, bank, dry cleaner's, etc. These are also the places where an uncontrollable crying jag is likely to happen. It seems that we prepare ourselves for our child's favorite places, but the most unexpected and mundane places can sneak up on you. The grocery store or Target were by far my most common triggers for a meltdown.

Seeing other people going on with their regular lives felt devastating. Didn't they know Austin was gone and I felt like the walking dead? I felt invisible at the grocery store. I felt like every person in that store had something I lost. Most importantly, they didn't even know it! They barked at their kids. Grabbed little arms to move them along. Ignored the crying toddler. Had sharp words for the questions innocently asked. It was excruciating. I know now it was probably exaggerated in my mind, but I felt like calling child protective services every time I stepped into a store!

My breath would catch if I rounded the aisle and someone had more than one kid in a shopping cart. Tears would threaten as I passed them, trying to smile at the kids. I couldn't meet a mother's eyes. Heaven forbid if the parent with those multiple children used an impatient or weary tone with those kids. I wanted to shake the parent and shout at them, "Don't you know that one of your kids could be gone tomorrow?!" I was a mess.

I had to learn some coping skills to get through the grocery store. Early on, I simply had to avoid times when kids would be at the grocery store. I started shopping early in the morning or later at night. Avoidance is a coping skill when you have this deep of a wound! As time passed, I could remember (with much regret and pain) that I too often said impatient or harsh things to my kids in grocery stores. I'm not sure when it started to shift, but eventually I started to have a bit more empathy for other parents trying to get through ordinary days.

> Seeing other people going on with their regular lives felt devastating.

One other coping skill was to remember how it felt to have people be impatient or rude to me just after Austin died. Those people had no idea what we were going through. I began to look at people in the grocery store and wonder what *they* might be going through. What if that mother I wanted to shout at just did lose a baby? What if that father had his four kids at the store because their mother just passed away?

On our grief journey, one way to get through the ordinary places during our everyday life is to remember that we are not alone. Others face horrific circumstances, too. People around us are walking through difficult days, just like us. Perhaps the difficulty might not be losing a child, but it might be a tragic loss just the same. Or, perhaps the person who is causing you to trigger into sad or mad has lost a child as well. What if that's true? Wouldn't you treat that person with renewed tenderness?

My tip for the regular places is to try your best to imagine the people you encounter as fellow sojourners who have also lost a child. A mindset like this helps me smile at people when I don't feel like it. The person I just passed could have lost their child last week, I think to myself. I force myself to look into her eyes and let her know that I see her. It's okay if you can't do this right now. Remember, it took time, lots of time. Years even. Try avoidance first!

What if it's not the people, but the place, the "stuff" that triggers your grief response? Oh friend, I have nothing but time for this problem. Pulling into Target without Austin in his car seat shouting, "Target!" with his little arms raised was enough to send me over the edge for quite some time. Give yourself some time, and allow yourself to leave the place when you need to do so. I used to force myself to stay, to go inside, to finish shopping, fighting or swiping at tears the whole time. Ticked off at life and everything. Mad as all get out. It didn't do one bit of good.

After a few disasters, I learned to just leave. It was okay. I just couldn't do it that day. It was never a life or death situation. Whatever I needed at Target or the grocery store could wait for a better day. You will have "good" days, bad days, and really bad days. Wait for a "good" day to tackle an ordinary place that is likely to trigger your grief. Yes, there will be some "good" days. You will reach a period of time when the "good" days become just a bit more frequent. Time, eventually, will smooth out this ragged grief (remember the shells?) and it won't be so tough to carry around every day.

I won't tell you that the grocery store or Target never triggers me after ten years. Both still do. Sometimes out of the blue (I hate that)! But, mostly, I get through both those regular places without incident. Without incident, perhaps, but never without at least one twinge of grief for some reason or another. I promised to be honest, and it hurts me to do it here, but you can probably already guess that you will have very few ordinary "grief-free" days anymore. Ask God to help you through each day, each minute. He will. Your grief will get lighter and smoother. I promise. You can do this! Keep putting one foot in front of the other. You must.

The Favorite Places

The favorite places of our lost child are the toughest of all. But if you have other children, you simply can't avoid the park, or the zoo, or the library. You must become superhuman. Seriously, that's how it felt early on. It took everything I had in me to take Ethan to those places that Austin loved. I don't even know who did it, but some sweet and strong soul took Austin's car seat out of the car. I don't even know when it actually happened. It helped, but it didn't remove the tear in my heart as I unbuckled only one child from his car seat for playing at the park. It felt so quiet in the car on the way to those favorite places. Sometimes, I would just turn around. Ethan was so little early on that he wasn't any wiser for it. Later, because time had passed and because I hated the fact that Ethan had to go to those places all by himself (without Austin), I would somehow gather superpower and force our way through the zoo.

All kidding aside, those superpowers came only by the grace of God. If I didn't spend about twenty or thirty minutes in the morning talking to God before Ethan woke up, I'm certain I would not have been able to make it through Austin's favorite places. You may feel just that way right now, like there's no way on EARTH you will ever be able to go to _____ ever again. I felt the same way. With God, however, all things are possible.

Yes, I know. If all things are possible with God, then why is my child dead? I know . . . and I don't know. What I do know is that God will comfort you if you let Him, if you ask Him. He will. God stands waiting for you to turn into His arms and let Him help you get through this nightmare.

I have no other tips for getting through your child's favorite places. Only God. I tried to think of something that could help you cope through this part, but I cannot think of one single thing. I pushed my imagination to be creative, think outside the box, for an idea, anything at all, to help another mom get through their child's favorite places. Nothing. I almost typed "I'm sorry," but I'm not sorry if this lack of

> If all things are possible with God, then why is my child dead? I know . . . and I don't know.

human help turns you toward God. He's my only answer, and with God you can overcome your grief and even enjoy your child's favorite places. It's a miracle, I know. I stand upon it every single day, in awe. God can do the same for you.

Your Home

My parents have this huge bulletin board where they have about a hundred pictures of their kids and grandkids. That space is covered with pictures of Jeff and Mark and Austin, along with the rest. They hung a special tapestry with all our pictures on the opposite wall. On the bookshelf in the dining room, more pictures. My parents want their missing kids' pictures everywhere.

In our house, you will find *one* three-picture frame with Austin eating an ear of corn in the top picture, both boys giggling and bumping foreheads in the middle picture, and baby Ethan in his lion costume in the bottom picture. That's it. It's on a wall we don't really see every day. We cannot handle pictures of Austin or Austin's things around our home on a day-to-day basis. Seeing his smiling face or his baby footprints in a Mother's Day gift is simply too much for us to bear every day.

This tip is easy: this is your loss. Do what works for you, being mindful of the others in your house. For example, I did put pictures of Austin up in my home office. Mostly, it's just me in here and it is here that I write and develop material to help others. It helps me sometimes to see his crazy-boy smile. Sometimes, it helps me keep my mind on the hope of heaven. I *will* see that smiling face again. I will. For all eternity and never missing him again for a single minute! Yet, even though he believes and knows these things, too, my amazing husband just can't see those pictures every day. Pictures and momentos rip open the wound for my husband (and a lot for me, too), so our home is very carefully arranged as far as our Austin pictures go. It works for us.

Feel free to figure out what works for your home. Remember to ask the others in your home how the pictures/momentos, or the lack of those things, might affect their grieving process. It took a while for Devin and I to have an open and honest conversation about moving some pictures and items into closets. When we took them down, we agreed, "at least for now, for a while." We've never wanted to put those items back out in the open. When we moved, those items moved, and when unpacking, it still felt too hard to see those things every day. Maybe someday we'll feel differently, but I doubt it.

On the flip side, my parents couldn't imagine going through the day without seeing those faces everywhere. I just want you to feel okay if you *don't* want that. Many people assume your house will have your child's pictures all over the place or that you will have erected some sort of wall or shrine. I want you to do what you think is appropriate, and be prepared to compromise with other loved ones who live in your home. I'll also go out on a limb and say that if family members *don't* live in your home every day, then they don't get a say in the house. It's also likely those family members are siblings of the lost child. I'm living proof that a sibling loss is not the same as a loss of a child. Losing a sibling is terrible and tragic. I hate it. Times two! But, if you are the mom and the other person is the sibling, your heart gets priority with regard to getting through the grieving process *for some things.*

Of course, there are other things that you simply must do as the mom of the living child/children. Your other children need you. Your other children desperately want you. If they still live at home, then they need to be part of the "house" conversation. If they still live at home, you'll have to do lots of stuff in this grieving process that would be easier if your children were grown. You'll have to buy Christmas presents, go school shopping, plan birthday parties, hide Easter eggs, etc., for one less child (seriously, can anything be worse?). How you decorate or memorialize your lost child in your home, however, needs to remain in the hands of those who must live in it every day.

Your Work

You may feel more pressure to keep things the same if you work outside the home. Your office or cubicle may have all kinds of kid pictures, kid drawings, even toys left behind in a drawer. I felt pressure to leave those things up in the office when Austin died. My pride and desire to look in control took precedence over my grief. It was as if changing my office to remove some Austin-related things would be seen as a sign of weakness . . . like a beacon of pity for all to see. No way. No chance.

I also must admit that I feared the judgment taking pictures of Austin *down* might bring from others. Does it look bad if a mother doesn't want pictures of her child up in the office? Can I leave the picture of Ethan up so I can see his baby face while I work? Are they going to judge me if I leave Ethan up and take Austin down?

I already felt "analyzed" every day I showed up to work after Austin died. I already felt like the topic of breakroom conversation. I did not want to add to that talk by doing anything people might think was weird. Please understand that I probably wasn't being analyzed or talked about, only that it felt that way to me. Grief caused me to be hyperemotional, which I wasn't used to. To say I was a bit sensitive after losing Austin might be an understatement. I was desperate to stay "the same" and not be looked upon with pity.

When I left that office and changed jobs, I was free to decorate in a way that soothed me at work. About two years after Austin died, I was able to put two pictures out of both the boys in different places. It felt just right. I could see them if I wanted to. I could talk about them if I wanted to. Their pictures also gave me openings to offer hope and perspective to people who came to my office. It was important to me that Austin's death would not be wasted, even a little bit. His smiling face in my office gave people a chance to ask, "Who's that?" or "Are these your boys?" Sometimes, I would just say yes and give their names (on bad days), but if it felt right, I would tell our story and allow Austin to bless someone with hope or new perspective.

If it's early in your grief journey and you are back to work, do what you need to do, and don't worry about others (easier said than done, but try). If you're back to work, you're doing great! If time has passed and those rough edges are getting smoother and your grief is a bit lighter, consider whether you

are ready to allow your story to bless someone else. You've
learned a lot on this journey already.

Family Gatherings

Austin died on April 25, 2008. Several months earlier, my
family had scheduled the first EVER Westrick family vacation. A house was rented for all of us, and our kids, to be together in the beautiful mountains of Colorado . . . in July 2008.
Since deposits and plans were made, Devin and Ethan and I
went on this family vacation. Big mistake. We simply weren't
ready. We weren't ready to be around my siblings with all of
their kids in the house. We weren't ready to enjoy gathering
without our child. The air in the house felt depleted for me.
I couldn't get my breath. I would often go to my bedroom,
exhausted. Do I want to play cards? Go for a walk? Play a game
with my nieces and nephews?

"Doesn't anybody realize that Austin's NOT HERE!" I
wanted to shout many times.

I didn't shout, but I wanted to the entire trip. At everyone,
but I didn't. I stuffed my grief deep down and did my best.
Devin drank, left to cry, and drank some more. Drowning his
pain in the bottom of a bottle, dealing with it as best he could,
while everyone else was on vacation. I barely noticed.

Years later, my family will still talk about what a great vacation that was, all of us together, in the beauty of Colorado. I
hardly remember the beauty. Whenever they mention it, my
gut wrenches a little bit. It had been so very painful for both
Devin and me. We should have stayed home.

With my keen understanding of the fact that we can lose our loved ones at any moment, you'd think that I would treasure a family vacation and be glad we went to spend time together. Nope. It was too soon.

Sometimes, you must care for yourself. You must admit that you are not, in fact, superhuman and able to continue on with family plans even now that your child is gone.

The next family gathering was on the Erickson side, in October 2008. This gathering was also planned before Austin died. It was a weeklong trip to an all-inclusive resort in Mexico, in celebration of Devin's parents' fiftieth wedding anniversary. The trip was easier for me because there were no kids invited. Only my in-laws, their three boys, and their wives. An adults-only, lie-by-the-beach vacation. This I could handle just a bit more. Devin, on the other hand, could not. He was with his brothers, at his parents' anniversary celebration. Austin would never sit around the table at a resort in Mexico to celebrate *our* anniversary. We would have years and years and years of anniversary celebrations without Austin. For that matter, all the travel and showing of the world that Devin wanted to do with Austin (his fellow adventurer) was lost forever. A trip with brothers was now something Ethan would never have again. Ethan would never get to race in the ocean or golf on its shores with Austin.

> We simply were not good at communicating what we needed during our deepest grieving season.

It was too much. Again, we should have stayed home.

Why did we go on these family vacations? Because we *do* know that death stands ready to snatch our loved ones without a moment's notice. Because we didn't want to hurt our loved ones. Because we were trying to *handle* our grief, for each other, for Ethan, for our families.

You will likely feel similar pressures—or guilt. Or determination. Even now, I can't really put my finger on why we felt compelled to go. It was only afterward that we realized that the cost on our hearts was too high.

As I type this, I think our families will be a little bit surprised to hear how much these trips took a toll on us. But we simply were not good at communicating how we were doing or what we needed during our deepest grieving season.

I encourage you to be more open with your family members about your pain. Of anyone, your family is best suited to support you and do their best to understand this loss. I also understand that may not be the case because families are so messed up sometimes! I know you might be tired of hearing it, but this is your loss, and no others can truly grasp it. So you have to communicate with them and then take steps to protect your heart.

If you have a significant family gathering on the horizon, consider whether you are ready to participate in it. If you have a sense of dread in your heart, then don't go. Make a phone call right now, and explain that this gathering will hurt your heart, will tear open the scab of losing your child. People will understand. If they don't, and they pressure you to attend (just for a little bit, won't you try, you can't stay home forever), gently say you love them and hang up the phone.

If you do decide to go, what you can do is prepare. Prepare your heart and mind for being with family. Remind yourself that your family cannot possibly understand how you feel because they (thank goodness) haven't lost a child. Prepare yourself to extend grace to your family members because they are not equipped to handle this pain and loss either. Everyone will feel awkward and unsettled for a while.

Prepare your heart for the familiar ache, and plan a response, even an exit strategy if you need one. If you begin to feel overly triggered, what will you do? Go to a different room. Take a walk. Clean the kitchen. Take a drive. Prepare at least one or two family members by telling them your plan. Next, let them know if you want them to join you in the response or exit strategy. Do you want company on that walk? Help cleaning the kitchen? Or, is alone time your best chance to lessen the pain? Communication is the key if you want help. Don't go it alone like we did!

Next Up: the Weird Stuff

The next few categories sometimes still surprise me. I hope they help someone out there!

Photographs

Looking at photos, taking photos, can send me into a grief response. Of course, you'd think looking at pictures of Austin might be a problem, and sometimes it is. Looking at pictures of my nieces, nephews, or friends, however, should not (in my opinion) trigger grief! It's dumb. I don't get it. Pictures make me cry. And sometimes, getting my picture taken can cause tears to well up. Ugh.

I've had some time to analyze this, so here's what I think about my photograph responses. Pictures are all I have left of Austin. Every picture I'll ever have has already been taken. There will be no more moments. No more begging him to sit still so I can get a shot. Also, getting my picture taken has the same meaning for me. Austin won't have these moments to smile and say "cheese" or "queso" as Ethan likes to joke. Capturing the memories or looking at the memories, it matters not. Both can sting my heart.

I don't have any suggestions for this thing that happens to me with regard to photos. I want as many pictures as I can get of Ethan and my other family members and friends. It just hurts. Not enough anymore that I avoid looking at or taking pictures, so with time it has eased quite a bit. If you have faced something similar or have your own "weird" stuff, I hope this helps you feel less alone. We are "weird" together!

Ambulances and Anxiety Attacks

This should come as no surprise, but it is still weird to me. Anxiety attacks feel scary. I never really knew how they felt until after Austin died. I don't think I even recognized the feeling as an "anxiety attack" early on. I just figured my panic at seeing an ambulance roaring down the road, lights flashing and sirens blaring, was a normal response after getting a call that one was at your house and tending to your child. I wasn't even home when the ambulance came through our neighborhood, and I never saw it. I arrived at the hospital after they had already transferred Austin and were trying to revive him in the emergency room. Yet an ambulance starts my heart to racing and my mind to praying, "I hope it's not a child. Lord, don't let it be a child. Please, God!"

Anxiety attacks are real, and don't let anyone else tell you differently. My sweet husband has been rushed to the ER several times, feeling and convinced that he was having a heart attack. After a few trips, we realized these attacks often came up in April or just after April. Grief response. Trigger gone overboard with no chance of stopping it. After realizing what it was and why it was happening, we started to treat it with medication that was designed for situational and occasional use. It works. No more frantic trips to the ER, which as you might imagine is a huge trigger for me. Medicine when you need it is way better than uncontrolled panic. Don't hesitate to tell someone what is happening to you. Ask your doctor. It may not even be forever. One day at a time, remember? Asking for help when you need it, okay? I pray that you will ask for and willingly get any help you may need. Sometimes, you can't pray it away. That doesn't make you weak. It doesn't make you less faithful or faith-filled. It just is what it is, at least for now. Praying and asking others for prayer is essential, but when it's not enough or soon enough, asking for help is the next step. Just do it!

Church

Just the place where you would think you might experience the most peace and healing, eh? Maybe, maybe not. Church can also be overwhelming. The music can be emotional. The stories can be sentimental or dramatic. Sometimes, the message makes you want to scream because you believed in God, and God let you down. You prayed, and it didn't work. How could church and praise and prayer help you now? Tears, sobbing, snot dripping . . . church. Sometimes it triggers me. Early on, sometimes I had to walk out. Today, walking out doesn't happen as often, but the tears and overwhelming presence of God drops me to my knees. Today, I more often cry because I feel the presence, power, and love of God. The songs move my heart in a love and joy response, to the point of tears. Sometimes, I still cry from a grief response, but not very often in church.

My relationship with God has grown through this grief journey to the point where I am certain that God is good and that He loves me more than I can imagine. That makes me weep because I don't deserve it from such a mighty and holy God.

Don't give up on God. Try leaning in instead of pushing away.

If going to church sounds awful to you, please consider spending time with God in another way. Even if you just cry or shout at Him, find a way to be in His presence. You don't have to go to church to do that! Eventually, I'd love to see you able to go back to church, to worship and serve alongside other believers. It's how we were designed. That being said, this losing a child pain might make corporate church too difficult. If that remains true for very long, try joining a small group where you can connect in a different setting. If you need to change churches because the memories at your "pre-loss" church are too painful to bear, then do it. Loving Christians should understand and support you in your efforts to worship and serve God in a way that works with your broken heart.

Whatever you do, don't give up on God. He's at work, even if you can't feel Him yet. Try leaning in instead of pushing away. Try shouting instead of ignoring. Try anything and everything until something happens. I'm certain God won't leave you this way. He won't. Give Him more chances to prove it.

Small Talk—Excruciating!

It wasn't until I joined a Facebook group for grieving parents (While We're Waiting) that I realized this one wasn't so weird! My husband and I have shared our newly found mutual dislike for making conversation many times over the years since Austin died. We would say these kinds of things either before or after a social event: *Do we have to go to this thing? I don't really feel like talking to people.* Who cares about any of that stuff people want to talk about? I just don't care about politics, the weather, sports, you name it! I don't like standing around trying to make small talk with people I don't know. What a waste of time. I'm not going to anything like that again. Ever.

Obviously, we aren't hermits in a mountain cave, so we are forced to act like civilized humans at certain times. But . . .

we don't like it anymore. It's weird. We used to be fun, social people who liked to go to dinners and parties, sporting events and shows. Now? Who cares? We are happiest at home or just the two/three of us together doing something. Adding other humans = ugh. Now we have to talk. It makes me giggle a little bit to write about this, because I read countless (think hundreds) of other parents lament over talking to people/making conversation/small talk after their child died.

I have tried to figure out why this is happening to us. After such a loss, we certainly realize that relationships are the stuff that makes life worth living. Yet the making of new relationships in a social setting is unbearable to many parents who've lost a child. I think it may be that in certain settings the conversation tends to be more shallow. I don't mean this in a bad way. It's just that you don't share your personal and deepest self in such a situation. Not that we want to talk about our deceased child, but we also might feel like an evening spent in such shallow interaction is kind of a waste of time in terms of eternity. Much of our focus is spent waiting to be reunited with our child, in heaven, for eternity. By comparison, the usual chitchat feels meaningless.

Also, some folks get wound up, "wrapped around the axle" as my father-in-law likes to say, about things that now seem unimportant to me. Football—really? Or people complaining about seemingly stupid things. Now that I've lost a child and faced my worst fear, my empathy meter is awfully low when folks complain about things that pale in comparison to losing a child.

I've been trying to work on this reaction. Many, many years have allowed me to dial back my irritation at complainers, but I still have to fight it. So, social setting conversation is difficult for me.

I know what you might be thinking: *but you talk to others as part of your ministry!* I lead small groups; I'm involved in women's ministry. How can I say that making conversation is difficult for me? Am I making this up? Nope. I wish that were true. How do I do it? Here I go again . . . prayer and time with God. I must spend time alone as well. I need time alone to recharge away from any conversation. Going to dinner after events I'm involved with is exhausting, especially if I've led any workshops or discussions about grieving. Talking about grief and Austin simply wipes me out. I've learned to build in a little time in the schedule to care for myself, to get alone and talk to God, to ask Him to help me be sociable with the women. I ask Him to help me stay engaged and find the words to make conversation.

If you're an extrovert, perhaps an inclination to avoid conversations and relationships will be easier to overcome in a shorter time. If you're a closet introvert like me, then may I encourage you with a pep talk I often give myself? It goes something like this: "God created us to be in relationship. Other people, community, and relationships are all designed by the Lord to help me. Plus, the enemy would like nothing better than to isolate me where he has a better chance to discourage me, lie to me, and keep me away from others who might be able to lift my spirits or turn me toward God. I will not let the enemy take advantage of me, so I will push myself to engage with others, pour something of myself out for my friends or those in need." Next, I pray something like this: "God, You know how I feel right now. Help me. Give my mind good thoughts and reasons for stepping out today. Lord, give me eyes to see and ears to hear what You want me to experience through others today. Give me grace upon grace, Father, to be a good friend. In the powerful name of Jesus, please grant me this help. Amen!"

If conversation or small talk has been difficult for you, I'd have to say, "Welcome to the club" again. Some tips to overcome this response:

- prepare your mind for questions that may come up about your child
- early on, take a good friend or two with you to act as a buffer, if needed
- remind yourself that others don't have the benefit of your perspective about life
- remind yourself that others have walked difficult journeys as well
- with your spouse, prepare a code word or exit strategy as a sign that it's time to leave
- stay by the buffet table and stuff your face (Kidding! We must laugh at ourselves, or we will drown in all our tears.)

Stress High = Grief High

It took me a couple of years to recognize this, so I am hoping to save you some time with this one. When stress in my life went up, my grief responses went up. If things were busy at work, I seemed to be more emotional. Anticipation of conflict or stressful meetings was sure to trigger a tough grieving day. About eighteen months after we lost Austin, I took on a new job where I had more responsibility and a team to direct. I became a wreck. Okay, more of a wreck. I wasn't sleeping. My hair was falling out. My stomach hurt all the time. Headaches were a daily thing, and migraines occurred at least three times a week.

> Add grief to a demanding job, and you have quite a load for one person.

Initially, I placed all of this on "stress." But it wasn't just from the new job. I had been in much more stressful jobs and situations before this one. I couldn't wrap my head around why I found this job so stressful. It was pretty much right on with regard to my skill set and strengths. Eventually, I figured out that it took very little stress to trigger my grief. I have no way to explain why it happens. When my job amps up, my grief takes me down. Not a good combination. I was not able to keep that job. I resigned and took a step-down job at a new location. In a more relaxed position, my grief subsided a bit. We also moved across the country, which helped force the healing process as well.

At this point, ten years into the journey, I am content to say that I can no longer work a highly stressful job. Perhaps, after such a loss and growing older, I am also less willing to spend eight hours a day in a pressure-filled environment. Likely, it's both.

If you are finding yourself maxed out in a way that feels like stress to you, I would encourage you to consider that it might actually be the grief that is flattening you. Grieving is exhausting work. Add grief to a demanding job, and you have quite a load to deal with for one person. Consider whether you can delegate more things in the near future. Consider whether your job suits the new you and your new life. Communicate with your team—let them know that your grief is causing you to feel more stressed, more on-edge. Ask them to have patience with you while you heal. Give *yourself* patience as you heal.

SPIRITUAL STEP:
Take Every Thought Captive

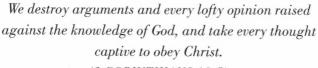

We destroy arguments and every lofty opinion raised against the knowledge of God, and take every thought captive to obey Christ.
(2 CORINTHIANS 10:5)

Getting through day after day, night after night, is probably the most difficult part of losing a child. The only way I have been able to make it through these past ten years without Austin is the idea of "taking every thought captive to obey Christ."

Taking charge of your thoughts is possible with God's help.

Swimming in sorrow and sadness is not from God. Jesus died so that we might be filled with divine joy, even in the midst of our grief (John 15:11; 16:20–24). God sent His only Son to die for you so "that in [Christ] you may have peace" (John 16:33). Jesus tells His disciples, "In the world you will have tribulation. But take heart; I have overcome the world" (16:33). Because I take the Word of God as pure truth, I believe these statements are true.

God wants me to have a joy-filled, peaceful life. He sent His Son to make sure it could happen. The enemy of my soul, however, would like nothing better than for me (a child of God) to remain broken, frozen, useless. Wallowing in the depths of my sorrow could happen so easily. There is no pain like losing a child. That cliché is true. But if I stay in the deep, dark pit of grief, then I feel like the enemy wins. Satan gets a mini-victory at my expense.

Oh, how my competitive and hard-headed nature hates the thought of the enemy getting anything he wants from me! I'm sure he danced a jig when Austin died. I'll never willingly give him one more reason to claim any sort of victory over me, my family, or my God. Not on my watch. The enemy underestimated me and my God. I won't give up trying to be joyful and peaceful because my Savior and Lord died to give me these gifts along with my salvation. I won't treat His gifts lightly; I will guard them with all the fierce love I can muster, each and every day. When I feel depleted and unable to lift my head some days, the gift of the Holy Spirit is ready to fill me up with strength again.

When dark thoughts and sadness want to run around in my mind, I say to myself, "Take every thought captive!" I remind myself that although our God understands and experiences sorrow, He remains a God of goodness, peace, joy, and love. The negative, self-pitying thoughts that can fill my head are not from God and the Holy Spirit. Those rewind moments of panic are not from a God who loves me, and thus, those thoughts must be from the enemy. As soon as I can recognize a thought as not coming from God, not one that God would want me to dwell upon, then I am able to fight. Hence, the "take every thought captive" battle cry.

When your mind wants to take control of your day and fill it with darkness and deep sorrow, recognize that as an act of the enemy of your soul and fight it with all you have left in you. Certainly, you will experience moments and times of sadness. But I am talking about those days when you feel as if you can't get out of bed. When you want to *remain* curled up in the fetal position on your floor, and you feel as if nothing good will ever happen again, cry out against the enemy and never allow him one more moment of victory over you. It is in these moments that you must fight the hardest to take one moment at a time, take one thought at a time, and try your best to control your mind. Do something to refocus on something positive. Refuse to give up!

Ideas:

- Recognize when your mind is running away from you into a dark place. Identify it as *not* from God, tell the enemy to go away, and ask God to fill your mind with His truth and peace.
- Find powerful images to represent the peace, joy, and love God has promised to you, and place them where you can see them often during your ordinary days.
- Create a collection of Scripture verses that remind you of the truth that you are a child of a good God (John 1:12; Acts 2:39; Rom. 8), that all good things come from God (James 1:17), and that you are filled with His goodness (John 14:16–17, 26–27).
- Make a list of three things you are grateful for, three things that prove you are loved, and three things that bring you joy.
- Create a collection of Scripture verses that speak power into your spirit, and then, when you feel exhausted and defeated, pull those verses out and allow the Holy Spirit to speak power and strength into your broken heart.
- Listen to Christian music. Allow the positive, God-focused music to drown out the darkness, and let the music fill in any gaps in your mind that want to run into the sadness.
- Identify anything in your ordinary days that trigger you; try to eliminate those triggers if you can.

- Keep a devotional within reach at all times so you can open it and refocus your mind on God and goodness; I have several in my home, and one at work, and for a long time I kept one in my car!

- If you can't stop the madness happening in your mind, force yourself to go outside. Try walking and looking at nature; let the details and beauty of creation remind you that God is with you—everywhere you go.

- Call a friend and confide that you are having a tough day; ask. Ask for help, and consider having a friend over to your house or even making plans to meet somewhere (so you are forced to get dressed).

- Exercise with praise music blaring! No way those dark thoughts can win over Jesus rock and roll and the endorphins released by exercise. The enemy has no power greater than the combination of praising Jesus and releasing endorphins!

From Devin Erickson,
Kim's husband and Austin's and Ethan's dad

dear wife-in-mourning:

How are you *doing* today? I ask how you are *doing* because your emotions are going to be all over the place from day to day. I had stronger words, but my wife wouldn't let me say them here. Your emotions cannot be trusted right now. Your emotions shift so many times in one day it makes you feel out of control.

How are you doing *today*? I ask how you are doing *today* because every day is different on this grief journey. Yesterday might have been a great day, but today you feel like you're losing it. Don't even think about tomorrow. Just do what you need to do today. Your function of being a wife, a mother, doesn't stop. You and your husband need to stay a unit, connected and working together.

My encouragement to you as a wife to a husband who has lost a child circles around your role in these areas: 1) your family; 2) as a couple; and 3) self.

Family

Don't forget that you're still a family. You were a family before your child died, and you remain a family today. Your family has changed, but you're still a family. This fact may be one of the very few things that doesn't change when you lose a child.

Whatever your circumstances, you and your husband have responsibilities in your family today. You have things you must do because you are the wife and perhaps the mom of other children. Those things still need to be done. Early on, Kim and I just simply did the next thing we needed to do. Laundry needed washing, groceries needed to be bought, and the weeds needed to be pulled. Kids needed to be cared for, fed, and helped with homework.

Even though everything is messed up in your world, you just need to keep going. Keep stepping forward. Your family needs you. As difficult as it is, this is our reality. Life just keeps going, and so must we. Just focus on today and the tasks in front of you right now. Try not to dwell on the past or project out into the future. Some memories from the past do more harm than good. Life does not offer a rewind button.

As your husband sees you going about what needs to be done, he'll feel relieved to do the same without feeling guilty about it. If you both stay focused on what the family needs, you have a shot at eventually getting to a place where the pain is a bit less and some joy returns to your family. As hard as this is, the old phrase, "it gets better with time," is true. Patience and understanding are going to play a huge part in your life from now on.

Your family will have a tough time getting back on its feet. The loss, the fact that your child is just . . . GONE . . . will leave such a big hole in your family. But, you're still a family. Work to stay a family! The last thing your other kids need right now is to sense a disconnect between you and your husband, or worse, for them to experience a divorce. You just can't pile more stuff on your other children.

So as you do those things you need to do for your family, one day at a time, next try thinking about you and your husband as a couple.

Couple

Don't forget that you're still a couple. You are still in love. You were a couple before your child died, and you remain a couple today. You and your husband remain. You still love and need each other.

Try taking little steps back to the things you did before your child died. Ease into it. Hold hands and take a walk. Watch a show you both enjoy on TV together. Hug tight for a moment. A kiss on the cheek and loving eye contact is still in you.

Yes, laughing again will jolt you at first and feel like you shouldn't. You can't imagine going on a date night with your husband right now. It's okay. Ease into it. You will get to a place where you will want to go on a date with him, laugh with him. Desire for each other will return. It will.

Do one little thing today that you used to do for him. Do it again tomorrow. Do another one next week. He's still the man you fell in love with and the one who loves you. You might not be able to feel the love now because so much has changed. Just don't forget that he's broken, too. Build each other back up. Little things at a time.

Life has changed, you both have changed, but the core strength of your relationship is still there. With patience and understanding, your marriage can be loving and good.

Self

You need to take care of yourself and allow your husband to take care of himself. He's going to need a lot of freedom right now. If your husband isn't a touchy-feely emotional guy, then don't poke the bear! No one likes to be poked. Don't insist that he talk to you about your child or how he's feeling. He'll talk when he's ready. Don't push him.

Resist the urge to try to help him. Don't get angry if he just wants to sit in front of the TV or take a nap or be silent. Even if it goes on for a week, let him handle this as he needs to. His grief will not come out like yours. Even though you've suffered the same loss, you won't grieve the same way or in the same timing.

It's like you're on parallel planes—traveling the same road, but going different speeds, looking at different things, noticing opposite sides of the road. Give him freedom to travel his own road at his own pace.

Know that every single relationship he has is being affected right now. Some guys, maybe most, are not good at emotional stuff, so take notice if his friends aren't calling him anymore. Your husband's friends are probably avoiding him, not inviting him out, wanting to avoid this huge emotional issue. Guys usually don't know what to say or do in those settings. So he might feel (and be) all alone.

Try sending him out to do something he enjoys. Let him do it by himself. Be understanding if he needs to step away from the family, whether for a few hours or maybe the whole day. By the way, these all apply to you as well. None of this is one-sided. You'll need to work together.

> At some point, your current life needs to take first place in your home.

I have two final bits of advice from our journey: 1) wean yourself off visual reminders of your child; and 2) get counseling sooner rather than later.

If there are lots of visual reminders of your child around your home, it might be difficult, but eventually consider slowly moving them to less obvious places. All the visual reminders might trigger your husband's grief more than he lets on. Make some compromises, if needed. At some point, your *current* life needs to take first place in your home. Your family will never EVER forget your child.

The memories will remain. There will be many reminders out there: songs, TV shows, even families standing in line at the grocery store. Allow your household to be somewhere your husband can heal by moving visual reminders to a more private place.

Maybe there's no one your husband feels comfortable talking to about this terrible loss. He might not talk to you. It's possible he won't talk to his parents or siblings. He may feel that talking to someone close to him about this loss means that he will be bringing sadness into the conversation. Even making small talk might be difficult now. It's just tough to talk to people. I've seen it on people's faces, the heartbreak and sympathy. It's too hard to be the cause of it by mentioning my child. So, please encourage him to talk to a third party, a pastor, a help line, a support group—anyone who can handle something like this without breaking down.

Encourage your husband (and yourself) to see a counselor, a professional who can offer you guidance during this time. It's not likely your husband has a mentor or an example to follow for this kind of thing. When he's having a bad day, he needs to have someone he can call. Let him know that it's okay to ask for help. Tell him you're proud of him for reaching out and taking steps to heal.

Your husband needs to be able to shout, cuss, hit something, or cry when he needs to—and he'll need to do all those things. Do what you can to set him up to let his grief out when he needs to and how he needs to. You are his strength through this, and he is yours.

Finally, remember this: your love is stronger than your loss.

All the love, strength, and bonds you shared in the years, months, even just days before your loss are still there. You can be happy again. Your husband can be happy again. Your marriage can be happy again.

Yes, it can.

The journey you are now on is going to be rougher, harder than it was "before," but take one day at a time. It is my prayer, my wish, that you find peace and comfort as the days go by. Be strong, patient, and understanding each and every day.

> Your husband needs to be able to shout, cuss, hit something, or cry when he needs to.

Steppin' forward,
—*Devin Erickson*

mourning and marriage

Your marriage might feel like you are scrambling around on the kitchen floor, picking up thousands of pieces of shattered glass. Just when you think you've got most of the pieces, you step on another shard. Meanwhile, you keep dropping more glass objects of your own. It's a mess. It's painful. It's dangerous. There are warning signs posted on your marriage, now and forever more: Be careful. Handle with care. Fragile. The person you love the most in this life, the person you gave your heart and your life to, is broken, shattered, and bleeding.

It's the worst when the love of my life is hurting more than imaginable, and yet there is nothing I can do. I feel like a spectator, unable to step into this horrible scene. The helplessness is bitter and so hard for me to handle. I don't like not being able to do anything to help the love of my life. Knowing the depth of his pain hurts my heart so much.

This is without question one of the hardest chapters for me

to write. Why? Because we're still in it. Losing Austin still affects our marriage to this very day. When you have two people in the house who are broken, it's not good! But I think we've survived because we *are* both broken. And we know it. We have tended to treat each other like fragile objects, capable of complete shattering at any moment. I pray that I can encourage you in your marriage, to keep fighting and to keep loving each other.

> The person you love most in this life, the person you gave your heart and your life to, is broken, shattered, and bleeding.

Your Marriage Will Survive . . . but How?

Your marriage will never again be without mourning. Your marriage will never be the same. Because you and your husband will never be the same, neither will your marriage. But just as you simply must pick yourself up and move forward one step at a time, so does your marriage. It will not happen all by itself. You must decide. You must become determined. You must be stubborn, never giving up.

My husband says that he prays every morning for these two things: patience and understanding.

Picture a person meditating and using a soft, drawn-out tone: patience and understanding.

Boy, does he need a ton of these to deal with me every day! Even our son jokes about it when tensions rise, even in jest, in our house. He'll put a hand on my shoulder and say, "Remember, Mom, patience and understanding." Then he backs away quickly, out of my swatting range!

In all seriousness, you must begin with the decision set in your heart that losing your child will *NOT* destroy your marriage. Period. End of discussion.

Now, how do we survive it? Let's start with some good news. You will hear over and over again that most marriages don't survive losing a child. Hogwash! It's not actually true. I've stopped correcting people and have learned to just smile and nod my head.

The statistical evidence actually shows that marriages involving the loss of a child survive at a *higher* rate than the average divorce rate. Our divorce rate is not what most people think:

> Like many myths, the high divorce rate one has snowballed way out of proportion. Harriet Schiff in 1977 (*The Bereaved Parent*) said that as high as 90 percent of all bereaved couples are in serious marital difficulty within months after the death of their child. She does not cite her source for this, and no one ever questioned her about it. So it became fact. Grief experts challenged the myth. By 1998 they said there was no evidence of higher divorce rates among bereaved parents.
>
> Then in 2006 The Compassionate Friends commissioned a survey, and one of the questions dealt with divorce. It was found that only 16 percent of parents

divorce after the death of a child, and only 4 percent said it was because of the death . . . that there were problems in the marriage way before the child died.[1]

If you've begun this journey thinking, "My marriage will never survive this," I believe you are in good company. It's fair to say that losing a child will provide enough ammunition to destroy your marriage. The good news is that it doesn't have to and it isn't "normal" or even the case in "most marriages." You have a say in this outcome. You couldn't change the outcome of your child's death, but you absolutely have choices and influence over how your marriage grows or bleeds through this process.

The key, in my opinion, is communication—and heaping helpings of grace, mercy, patience, and understanding. Assuming your husband is also the father of your child, he is the only other person in the whole world who has the same wound as you. He is hurting as much as you are right now. While his relationship to your child might have looked different than yours on the outside, he also had his heart shattered into a thousand pieces and will be forever missing a piece of his soul.

When the boys were little and I had a tendency to tell Devin how to do something with them (like providing a meal, giving them a bath, or putting them to bed), he would remind me, "I've been doing this parenting thing as long as you have, you know!" It became our way of signaling when I

1. Sandy Fox, "Divorce Rate among Bereaved," Open to Hope, August 4, 2009, https://www.opentohope.com/divorce-rate-among-bereaved/.

was micromanaging his dad-role. It was a signal to back off and let him be the dad.

May I encourage you to remember that your child's father is a parent, just like you? (Please know that I would also include stepparents who have been like a parent to the lost child. My brother, Mike, is a stepdad, but he never thinks of himself that way, and neither do I. He is as much a dad to Andy and Stacy as any biological father.) He had hopes and dreams that have been ripped from him. Never forget that he is the dad. Broken and battered just like you. I often pray for God to give me eyes to see my husband as Jesus sees him. I ask Him to show me my husband's best qualities, his deepest hurts, and his unmet needs and desires. I ask for the Holy Spirit to allow only words that will build my husband up, never tear him down.

> May I encourage you to remember that your child's father is a parent, just like you?

It's easy to see and feel the things that are annoying, or even hurtful, when we are grieving. We are not ourselves. In the previous chapter, I told you when my stress goes up, my grief does as well. I think the next effect is that my marriage begins to show some cracks and rough spots. Stress can make any marriage susceptible to trouble, and grieving a child is super stressful.

You are already on edge, you are tired, and you have all your heart can handle without picking up his dirty socks or fixing something you asked him to do months ago. Don't even get me started on situations where *he* is irritable and taking it out on you. Worse yet are those times when he is silent for what seems like days because he is so sad. I begin to feel like I've done something wrong or angered him in some way. It's not true, but it's how I feel so I get defensive or silent back. Triggers are everywhere!

It's so easy to allow harsh attitudes to come out toward your husband. He's the "safest" person right now to whom you can let out some of your feelings. He promised to love you and keep you for better or worse, right? So true. But, the same applies for him. You are his "safest" person, and you also swore a covenant to him, forever and always, no matter what.

One of the best things you can do for your marriage right now takes only one moment: *commit*. Set your mind on saving your marriage. Push negative thoughts about your marriage aside. Be determined that your marriage will survive and will be stronger than ever. Strive for the mindset that losing your child will bring you closer together. Take every thought captive about your husband and your marriage by focusing on only positive things. Do not let grief lead to anger or bitterness between you. Be determined and committed with regard to your marriage, and be devoted to your husband.

With those promises in mind, there is another statement you will hear over and over again: everyone grieves differently. This statement happens to be 100 percent truth. We do all grieve differently. You and your husband will undoubtedly handle grief differently, perhaps as different as night and day. Or, if you are lucky, perhaps only as different as twilight and dark. Perhaps you and your spouse will share the same mind with many of the grieving tasks that are now a part of your marriage. Either way, this much is true: you need to talk to him about it. You need to discuss your feelings and listen quietly to his needs or desires when it comes to grieving or remembering your child.

So often, I did not discuss Austin with Devin. I did not let Devin know when I was having a particularly bad day. In fact, I usually try (even today) to hide my bad days from him. I don't take my own advice here! I don't want to add to his already unbearable grief. I don't want to become another weight around his neck. If he's having a good day, I don't want to bring him down. If he's having a bad day, I don't want to make it worse. So, most times, we didn't/don't talk about Austin at all. Luckily, we were (and still are) on the same page with the "big stuff" regarding Austin and the grieving landmines in our lives.

Some "big stuff" items to discuss and "landmine" questions to ask are:

- How do you think we should handle his/her birthday? Do you want to do the same things, or different things? (Or, like Devin and me, *no* things!)
- Would it help you to handle packing up his/her things right away or a bit down the road?
- Do pictures help you or hurt you right now? What would you like to do about his/her pictures, if anything?
- Will you please tell me when you are having an unusually tough day? How can we communicate to each other that the grief is high today?

- Are there items that you feel especially tied to our child that you want to keep? Do you want to display those items in our home or your office? Or would you rather those items be stored out of sight for now?
- What do you want me to do when you break down? Hold you? Give you some space? A little of both?
- How do you want to handle the anniversary of his/her death? Do you want to do something special to address it? Or, do you just want to get through the day quietly and as quickly as possible?

These are just a few of the specific items that can create issues in your marriage. There are probably others. In addition, there are probably other things about your marriage that were "issues" before you lost your child. It's not like those things have magically disappeared. The things that drove you just a little nuts before your child died might cause a major meltdown now. Vice versa is also true: the things you could ignore before might take on importance now.

Bottom line: you'll have to discover who your husband is *now*. You'll have to figure out who you are now. You'll have to be patient while you both try to figure that out. You have to be willing to adjust your expectations of each other for a long while, maybe for the rest of your lives.

Will you ever enjoy a date night again? Laugh together? Yes, you will.

Will you ever enjoy sex again? Yes, you will. It might be

weird and feel weird, especially during those first several months, but lovemaking and fun will return to you and your husband. It might take time, so be patient. More importantly, don't feel guilty about it. Don't feel guilty about not "feeling like it," and don't feel guilty about enjoying it! Like everything else in your life, things have changed. It may take some time to find your way through the new dynamics.

The good news is that your marriage can be deeper and stronger every single day. Your confidence in your love and your husband's love can be a deep well from which to pull more strength for the hard days. If both of you can treasure the fragile people you've become, then there can be such sweetness between you. Your marriage can become stronger than ever, a steady place of refuge from the grief you both carry.

SURVIVAL STEP:
Commit and Communicate!

As discussed above, the first step is committing to your marriage. Set your mind on surviving. Be determined that you will revive your marriage every time it takes a dip.

Next, as painful as it might be, talking about grieving with your husband is a necessary step in surviving your loss with your marriage intact. If he's like most men I know, he won't want to talk about it. So choose wisely your times to have a talk about the above topics. During the middle of the big game is *not* a good time! Right after work is *not* a good time! In the midst of an argument about something else is *not* a good time! Pick your timing!

Please know that you'll need to communicate and adjust many times. Just like any marriage, it will change and grow. Toss in grieving, and you have more things that are changing with the passage of time. As the initial shock and first stages of grieving wind down, new issues will come up. For example, as Ethan entered T-ball when he was about five years old, our hearts hurt so much because we knew he should have had an older brother to play with in the yard. The lack of a brother for Ethan became more painful as time went on. Now that Ethan is in middle school, there is a gaping hole in our lives again. We need to adjust to Ethan not having siblings like both of us had to lead, guide, and tease our way through adolescence.

And the tenth year without Austin hit me particularly hard. Perhaps it is because I was writing this book, but I recall that my mom also had a difficult year when the ten-year anniversary of my brother's car accident came around. There will be things that you just don't anticipate or expect, for yourself and for your husband. Expect the unexpected! Make sure the communication lines are open and you are expressing your new and changing needs as time passes.

SPIRITUAL STEP:
Pray . . . a LOT!

Shortly after Austin died, while we were still really new in our church and young in our faith, the pastor and his wife were taking a lot of time with Devin and me. Pastor Steve led me to what is now called my "wife verse" when I was trying to "help" Devin along with his faith journey or his grieving. Since I tend to try to "help" Devin along with many things, this verse is so critical for me and for our marriage.

Before you read it, may I ask you to set aside any desire to reject these ideas because it sounds like you must become a doormat? A "submissive" wife does not mean that your ideas or feelings are not as important as your husband's, nor does it mean that your husband controls everything. Being submissive does mean respecting your husband as a man. Every man wants respect. Just like every woman wants to be loved by her husband, every husband desires his wife's respect more than anyone or anything else. With that in mind, please read this verse and then let me show you how I pray it:

Likewise, wives, be subject to your own husbands, so that even if some do not obey the word, they may be won without a word by the conduct of their wives, when they see your respectful and pure conduct. Do not let your adorning be external—the braiding of hair and the putting on of gold jewelry, or the clothing you wear—

but let your adorning be the hidden person of the heart
with the imperishable beauty of a gentle and quiet spirit,
which in God's sight is very precious.
(1 PETER 3:1–4)

You see, it's not my words that can strengthen my husband's faith journey or lessen his grief—it's my behavior. If I want to see Devin grow in his faith, then I need to show him how I am growing in mine. Growing faith means growing more like Jesus. Growing more like Jesus means giving more of myself for others, loving others more than myself, and having a servant's heart. So, I pray for the men in my family to be "won over" by my behavior and not my words (because I'll keep those to myself).

I hope I'm not the only wife who sometimes thinks that my marriage would be better if I were more attractive. If I lost ten pounds and got in better shape, then I'm just certain my husband would ask me to go on a date night! Or maybe he'd open up to me if he saw me trying so hard to look good. It's dumb. I know it's not true. I still have these thoughts sometimes. My "wife verse" helps me to remember that what my husband loves about me is . . . well . . . me. Just me. Who I am on the inside, warts and all.

What I really should focus on is developing that "imperishable beauty of a gentle and quiet spirit." I want imperishable beauty! Seriously, fighting gravity and wrinkles is hard. Again, I don't take this verse to mean that I allow my husband to walk all over me and just keep quiet about it. To me, this verse means that I am more beautiful to my husband when my "hidden person of the heart" is gentle and soft-spoken. When peacefulness rules in my heart, I am more attractive. Now, these are not my natural traits, so this takes prayer. I ask God to fill me up with peace, gentleness, and a quiet/settled spirit. Every. Single. Day. Not kidding.

Finally, I pray about that last line, about how wives with quiet and gentle spirits are "precious" in God's sight. "Precious" has taken on new meanings these days. We tend to use it when we see something cute, like kittens or babies. I never wanted anyone to say about me, "Well, isn't she precious." I was a tomboy, an athlete. I did not appreciate anything "precious." Great news—that's not what the writer of this verse meant!

The original word used in this verse meant precious like a precious gem, a rare stone, a thing of great value. Now we're talking, right? As women, we want to be needed, to be of great value. This very need is at the heart of my trying to "help" Devin along with his faith or grief. But this verse tells me that if I am to be of great use, of great value to God, then a gentle and quiet spirit is best. I want to be of great value to God. I want to have a spirit and behavior that the Lord can use in our home.

So, I pray most mornings for a spirit toward Devin that is of great value to the Lord. Instead of trying to help my own way, I ask God to settle my spirit so that an inner beauty that only comes from Him will draw Devin and Ethan closer to the Lord, that my behavior would be of great value to Him. My prayer usually sounds as simple as this:

Lord, help me close my mouth. Let Devin and Ethan be drawn to You by my behavior. Let my beauty come not from outward adornments, but from Your Holy Spirit. Lord, fill me up with that quiet and gentle spirit that is of great value to You.

There are many other books and resources for strengthening your marriage and praying for your husband. I heard one pastor recommend that husbands and wives should read at least one "how to improve your marriage" book a year. His point was that our marriage is something of vital importance to us, so we should be able to carve out enough time to read one book about it per year. I like this idea, but must admit that I haven't hit the one per year mark . . . yet.

I have read the following books and found them very helpful for our marriage:

- *The 5 Love Languages* by Dr. Gary Chapman (Northfield Publishing, 2015)
- *For Women Only* by Shaunti Feldhahn (Multnomah Books, 2013)
- *Laugh Your Way to a Better Marriage* by Mark Gungor (Atria, 2008)
- *The Power of a Praying Wife* by Stormie Omartian (Harvest House, 2014)

sibling sadness and (yes) rivalry

So much of my sadness about losing Austin is wrapped up in Ethan. So much so that I hope Ethan never reads this book. It is the groaning cry of my heart that he never has any need of the advice in this book. In addition, I don't want Ethan to feel some sort of responsibility for my sadness. Mostly I hide it from him. I can probably count on one hand the times when he has seen me cry about Austin.

Ethan was only fifteen months old when Austin died at the age of three. I didn't cry in front of Ethan in the beginning, because you know how babies get when their moms cry. They can't take it. It makes them cry. As he grew out of that phase, I still felt so much sadness that Ethan no longer had a brother, or any sibling, that I just couldn't bear adding my sadness to his little life. I became determined that I would not add to his burden, nor add to his sense of loss. He had already lost his brother, so I wasn't about to let him lose his mom either.

Someone said to me once, "You know, Ethan only has one mom, so you better take care of her!" Since this rang true for me, I knew that I couldn't let losing Austin destroy me for Ethan. Curling up in the fetal position on my bathroom floor was not an option. Sitting in sadness instead of taking sweet Ethan to the park was not fair to him. Ethan deserved a beautiful childhood. He didn't deserve to lose his only brother, any more than we deserved to bury our child. It stinks for all of us.

The only part of this horrible situation I could control was how I would handle this crushing loss in terms of being a wife to Devin and a mother to Ethan. Everything else was out of my hands. Yet I could set my mind on being the best wife and mother I could be. It was this determination, I believe, that helped stabilize my marriage and Ethan's childhood. I was dead set on *not* letting the loss of Austin destroy Ethan's childhood.

A big part of any child's coming-of-age experience is the marriage of his/her parents. Children have an uncanny sense of tension in the home. They can smell an argument brewing better than any hunting dog. For these reasons, my determination with regard to my relationship to Devin also became fierce. There was no way I was going to let Ethan lose "us" too. Not gonna happen. Nope. No way. We were still going to be a family, even if it would never be whole again. I would do everything in my power so that losing Austin did not destroy everything Ethan knew about his life so far (see the Mourning and Marriage chapter).

But. Despite all of my efforts, and even though he was too young to understand it, Ethan was and still is impacted by our loss of Austin in 2008. In fact, whenever anyone asks him about his siblings, he promptly tells them that he had an older brother, but he's in heaven now. How's that for your first parent-teacher meeting? All the grown-ups paste a smile on, and everyone who hears it says they are sorry for your loss. All the while, Ethan has no idea that he dropped a bomb because I am determined to shield him as much as I can. I feel like it's

> There was no way I was going to let Ethan lose "us" too. We were still going to be a family.

the least I can do for him. I can hold it together and not fall apart. I never want him to think that something he said or did made me sad. I never want him to shoulder any of my grief.

As far as our day-to-day life went, Ethan often asked for stories about Austin. He still sometimes ask questions about Austin: do you think Austin would like this book? Do you think Austin would like to play baseball? Who do you think would run faster, me or Austin? Did I learn to talk before Austin did?

You get the idea. Sibling rivalry apparently survives even death! Even if your other children have no true memories of the child you lost, he or she can feel that sibling rivalry kick in. I think we have to be very careful as the mom to make sure we don't idolize the child we lost or make her look like a saint to our other kids. Sometimes I would tell stories where Austin threw a toy or a temper tantrum and had to go into "time out" just to make sure I wasn't putting some false picture of Austin into Ethan's head. I am still trying to make sure that I don't put Austin on some sort of pedestal in our family. Austin should never take on more importance than Ethan. Just like you strive to make sure all your kids know you love each of them as much as the others, you'll need to be sure that your surviving children feel that equality now.

> I think we have to be very careful as the mom to make sure we don't idolize the child we lost or make her look like a saint to our other kids.

One thing I hope we did well for Ethan was not allowing Austin or his things to be "untouchable." The things I wanted to hold precious as "Austin's" I put into a box in my closet. If I didn't want to take the chance that Ethan would break something or lose something, it went into the "Austin Keep" bin. Otherwise, he could play with those toys, color in those books, ride that tricycle. He was allowed to play on the bunk beds (before we donated them) in Austin's room and throw Austin's stuffed animals from the bottom bunk to the top and back down again. Yes, it sliced my heart open most days, but remember I was determined to give Ethan the childhood he deserved. So far, that meant getting his hands on Austin's things or hand-me-downs. He loved it, so I had to allow it.

Your other children will love getting their hands on your lost child's things, too. If they are old enough, certain things will hold memories for them, too. It will be important for your surviving children to hold on to a few special items as well.

Perhaps each sibling should have their own "keep" bin. I put several things into the "Austin Keep" bin that I plan to pass on to Ethan one day. But, if he were old enough to have his own memories, then I would let him have his own "keep" bin.

Another idea is to make a photo album for each of your surviving kids, filled with photos of them with their lost sibling. I made a little photo album of pictures where Austin and Ethan were together, and especially chose the ones where Austin was touching Ethan or holding him. I made it for Ethan, but it turned out to be for me! Some days that little photo album was the only thing that helped me go on one more day. I could look at those pictures and think, "Someday, when we get to heaven, I'll have all of eternity to see my boys together just like this, forever and ever."

Someday, I'll pass that little photo album on to Ethan. For now, I find that I still need it sometimes. In fact, now that I am thinking about it, making that photo album was one of the most difficult things I ever did in those early years. Looking back, may I encourage you to ask a good friend to do this task for you? Tell her what kind of pictures you'd like to see fill that album and leave the rest to her. Ask her to put one together for you, too, so you don't have to hijack one of your kid's albums like I did!

Today, as I write this chapter, Ethan is twelve years old. Practically a grown man, if you ask him. He's a mature, responsible young man already. He loves to read, play sports, and watch movies. Ethan is a normal, growing, almost-teenager. Since he's the only child we have living at home, he likes to say he "lives under a microscope" (a phrase he took from a book we read and that he declared to be true of his life!), but we try to let him be a normal kid as much as possible. Devin and I take as many opportunities as we can to create memories with Ethan. Losing Austin has made our relationship with Ethan, and our family time, so much sweeter. Even a family movie night is a treasure! I think it's fair to say that Ethan is having a great childhood, despite missing out on having an older brother. While he feels the loss sometimes, I think he mostly just carries on with life and growing up. It's kind of amazing to watch!

Since there are so many variables as to situations and other children, I am at a bit of a loss for more advice for you and the other children in your family. However, since I am not only a mom-in-mourning, but also a sibling-in-mourning, perhaps I can tell you of my experiences in losing my two brothers. I can tell you that losing a sibling is not as difficult as losing a child. Losing my brother Jeff in a car accident when he was twenty-three and I was nineteen was terrible. About eight years after Austin died, losing my brother Mark to brain cancer after four, hard-fought years, was like slicing all my grief wounds open at once. It is still especially difficult whenever I see one of his four kids or his wife.

Yes, losing a sibling is a tragedy, and I don't want anyone, especially my Ethan, to have to walk through it. That being said, it cannot compare to the loss of your own child. The grief our surviving kids must bear will not feel like *this* loss.

Time will heal them. Memories will become sweet, without

the bitter sting that accompanies the loss of a child. Their lives will return to a "normal" feeling at some point. But, you never have to worry that they will forget their sibling. They will treasure all their memories and good times. Do I miss my brothers? Terribly! Do I hate that we spend holidays without them? Always! But the deep, soul-changing pain that comes from losing a child does not accompany sibling loss for the rest of their lives. In the beginning and during the first several years, the sibling pain is sharp and so difficult. Yet, time softens and lessens the pain of sibling loss.

At least we have these facts to comfort us when we think of our other children without their sibling. Their grief will most definitely get better!

Also, I love the book *Heaven for Kids* by Randy Alcorn (Tyndale, 2006) to help you talk to your kids about what happens when we die, what heaven might be like, etc.

SURVIVAL STEP:
Don't Build Any Pedestals

As both a sibling and a mom, the most damaging thing I think a grieving mom can do is put the child she lost up on a pedestal. Your other kids need you now more than ever. Your surviving children need the best mom you can be right now. I'm sure you don't need me to tell you to soak up every single minute you have with your remaining children because you never know when that time is going to end. So, don't spend precious time with your living children in despair or in the past. Create new memories. Start new traditions. Give your kids the best childhood that you can (which, by the way, also means solid discipline, boundaries, chores . . . but that's a whole other book!).

Remind your kids that the one who died was not perfect. Pepper in stories of bad choices and lessons learned. Don't forget that sibling rivalry exists, even though their sibling doesn't live on earth anymore. Try to make sure you compliment them as often as you talk about the child you lost.

SPIRITUAL STEP:
Give Them Back to God

Before I could move forward in my relationship with God, I had to forgive Him for letting Austin die. I know this is probably not a sound theological idea, me forgiving God, but it's the truth for me. I had to wrestle the idea of a loving and good God with a God who would let Austin die, shatter me and Devin, and make Ethan an only child. It just wasn't fair. I thought that I was a pretty good person. I didn't commit any of the really big sins. I worked hard, was honest, tried to be a good wife and mom, so why did *my* kid have to die? Where's the good God in that?

How do you forgive God for allowing your child to die?

While I was ranting, my thinking went something like this: why do the "bad" people I see all around me get to keep their kids? Why are these people who do terrible things the ones who get to have sixteen children? There are people who murder and molest, and *their* kids didn't die! Why would a good God who supposedly loves me allow *this* to happen to me and my family?

Does this sound like your thoughts sometimes? So how do you forgive God for allowing your child to die?

It's not easy, but it is simple: you give your children back to God. They all belong to Him. Everything under heaven was made by God, for God. You and your children exist only because God created and sustained your every breath. Austin, sweet and funny Austin, came out of me and into this world because God knit him together in my womb and added an extra dose of ornery just for fun. The amazing Ethan rides his bike to school and plays ball in the yard with the neighbor boys because God deems it just so.

Nothing we have or experience belongs to us. Austin was never mine to begin with. Austin was "on loan" to me from God. Since I can't even bake a cake without messing it up, I can't think of telling the Creator of the universe how to run His kingdom. If He wanted to take Austin to heaven after three years, it was His prerogative.

Now, this kind of thinking didn't come easy. It took a lot of time reading and studying my Bible before I decided that everything written about God in that Bible was true. Of course, I have no tangible proof that it's true. If we were in a court of law, the evidence would be considered circumstantial at this point. That being said, just like a good jury, I have pondered the questions and reviewed what evidence I did have in front of me for a long time.

I have come to the conclusion that God is good, that He created everything in our universe, that He sustains and provides for us, and that He continues to rule and reign over our world. The Bible is my evidence that God always keeps His promises, and He always does what He says He's going to do.

As a result, I bow my will to His. Whatever God directs or allows to happen in my life is under His authority, not mine. I am merely a steward, a caretaker of the people and things He allows me to have in this world.

It is this very same thinking that allows me to remain somewhat sane when it comes to Ethan and my fear of losing another child. Ethan is not mine; He belongs to God. If God wants Ethan to live, he'll live. If God calls Ethan home to heaven (Ethan accepted Christ at four years old, on a Good Friday), then I'll just have to wait to see him there. There's no need to worry and fret myself, my husband, or Ethan into a tizzy. Worrying over our children does no good. They are in God's hands. Because they are in God's hands, praying does work! How do I know? The Bible tells me so! Jesus prayed for Peter, that Peter would return to serving the Lord after denying Him three times: "Simon, Simon, behold, Satan demanded to have you, that he might sift you like wheat, but I have prayed for you that your faith may not fail. And when you have turned again, strengthen your brothers" (Luke 22:31–32). And, of course, Peter did 'turn again.'

Instead of hovering and fretting over your remaining children, give them back to God. Open the hand that tries to clutch tightly onto your kids in a desperate attempt to control their lives. Hold the blessing of each child in an open hand, lifting them up to God. As you lift them, try telling God you trust Him for reclaiming the one who is no longer with you. Keep doing this in your mind until your heart feels it. It may take a few years, but I'll pray you get there because there is such peace and freedom and hope when you place your children in the hands of the almighty God.

Chapter 12

I have to do this the rest of my life?

When you begin to feel as if you might live through this, when you are able to get through some ordinary days, a new realization might begin to creep into your heart. As you go about your regular day, suddenly it occurs to you: I have to do this for the rest of my life. For the remaining thirty, forty, even fifty years, I have to do life without my child. Seriously?!

You have been fighting so hard to get your feet underneath you. The battle to get up and get dressed every day was difficult. You were so determined to get your life back into some kind of routine, perhaps give some feeling of "normal" to your other kids or spouse. You were just starting to feel like you might not die from this pain in your heart. The trip to the mental hospital for a very long stay no longer feels like a good option to you. Things are settling into a semblance of a routine.

And then it hits you. The stretch. The long, long stretch of the years you have left on this planet. That feeling like you can't possibly live through this returns with a vengeance. You might be able to hold it together for a year or two, but not decades. No way. Can't happen. I don't have the strength for the next fifty years. I'm so tired already. Please, God, don't let me live a long life!

You mean it. Your mind cannot comprehend living so long without your child. Your soul can't fathom the stretch of life on this planet. Most likely, you are not suicidal. You are just exhausted.

Remember, grieving is hard work. Getting up every day and putting one foot in front of the other is going to wipe you out for a very long time. But remember that your grief *will* get smoother and lighter, and the days will pass with less effort with every sunrise and sunset.

After several years, when you start to feel somewhat normal (for the most part), the stretch will rear its ugly head again. Once you start gliding through most of your days (and you will eventually), the years and years remaining will bring a hopeless feeling back into your soul. So, what do we do? Crumble after all these years? Give up trying? I know, it sounds a bit tempting, but you won't do it. You've come this far, and you are not willing to slide back into the ugly, dark pit of grief again. You won't allow yourself to go that dark again.

That's the good news. Once you are well enough to start feeling the stretch, you are well enough to fight against the dark. The only bad news is that the stretch remains the stretch, as far as I can tell. Ten years into my grief journey, thinking about the stretch is something that can turn my heart cold or ignite self-pity.

As time continues, your other children reach milestones that your missing child would have enjoyed. Family moments and gatherings remind you that everyone else is continuing to grow and experience new things while your child is frozen at the age they died (as far as memories on earth go). Maybe like me, your family continues to encounter difficult circumstances—even more death. My brother Jeff died in a car accident when he was twenty-three (in 1989), Austin died from complications with strep throat in 2008, and my brother Mark died from cancer in July 2017, the year I began writing this book.

You might think that would be enough for our family, eh? Yet, on August 25, as we were trying to get through Mark's birthday without him, we were holding our breath as we awaited biopsy results for my sister. The test came back positive. My sister was diagnosed with breast cancer on my recently deceased brother's fifty-fifth birthday.

Life in the stretch . . . seriously? It's too much sometimes, especially when other losses and difficulties pile up on top of our grief. Other senseless tragedies can also cause the stretch to spin me into a bad day. As I was writing this book, fourteen teenagers were killed in a school shooting just hours from my house. A three-year-old was killed in a road rage shooting. Twelve children were found tortured by their parents. Really, God? I really want God to blow the trumpet and kick off the apocalypse. Not kidding. I'd be willing to bet most parents who've lost children are more impacted by the stories in the news than other parents. It's all so senseless, and you're often still so tired from living while grieving. Let's do this thing about the end of times. It's a mess down here. Let's go. Am I right?

Life: a Breath

Since we don't have control of the matter, my suggestion is to remember that this life is just a breath. Life on earth is a mere shadow, a passing vapor, when compared to eternal life. Our eternal lives are forever, infinity. We can't really wrap our minds around forever, and ever, and ever, and ever . . . and this world is tangible and present. It's easy to get wrapped up in the things of this world because it is right here and now. But that is not the human story. Humans were created for eternal life with God. Our longing for eternal life was given to us by our Creator. Every human heart has an empty spot that can never be filled outside of God. It's what we're waiting for. It's why the stretch feels so very long. Our lost child is not the only thing that caused the void in our heart or our heartbreak at the tragedies of this life.

How do I know for sure that God exists and that eternal life in heaven is coming next? Because God said so. You might think that I believe heaven exists because of my moment when Austin passed when I felt him say into my heart, "But Mom, it's so pretty here." That moment is part of it, but it wouldn't have sustained my lawyer mind for long. I would have found a way to brush that moment to the side as a mother's longing heart.

Over time, if that was all I had, I would have talked myself out of the reality of that moment. Wishful thinking, a mental break, or a fantasy made up in my mind because I couldn't comprehend reality. All things my lawyer mind and skeptical attitude about religion would have agreed with at the time.

What changed? I believe that when I accepted Jesus as my Lord and Savior, I received the gift of the Holy Spirit. Why do I think the things Jesus claimed to be were true? Why do I claim the gift and power of the Holy Spirit? For the same reason I believe in eternal life: because God said so.

If you accept Jesus as Lord and Savior, the Holy Spirit then fills you, and then when you pick up the Bible seeking the truth about God, you will see it, too. You will find, if you read the Bible for yourself, that God has this habit of doing what He says He's going to do. Over and over again, whenever a human has recorded something God said He would do, eventually, God does exactly that.

It is the fact that God does what He says He's going to do, never wavering from His Word, that causes me to trust Him. Everything about me, my family, my life is entrusted into His mighty hands because He is worthy of that trust. So there simply must be a heaven and eternal life because God said that heaven and eternal life await His people. God said He would send a Savior, one who would grant eternal life to those who believe in Him. He did. He sent Jesus. Jesus said He would rise from the grave in three days time. He did. God said He would establish a new heaven and a new earth that will last for eternity. He will.

It's really that simple for me. Not because someone else told me so. Not because I was raised to believe it. Not because my broken heart wishes for it. Rather, I believe it because I've read it with my own eyes, pondered it with my own mind, and grasped it with my own heart. The things recorded in the Bible really happened, and each time God made a promise, He kept it. Period. End of story for me.

As a result, I live through this life with the attitude that life is so short in comparison to eternity. This world cannot compare to the glory of heaven, where I will spend *way* more time than I did on this earth. Thank goodness!

Let me share with you my first glimpse into the reality that God does what He says He's going to do, that God keeps His promises. One day, during my very first reading through Genesis, I was reading about Noah and the flood. The people of Noah's time were so evil that God was sorry He ever created mankind. He asked Noah to build the ark to protect only Noah's family and two of each animal. Next, God wiped it all out. Everything on earth, humans and animals alike, was swept away by a flood that engulfed the entire planet. Gone.

When the rain stopped and the flood subsided, Noah and God had a conversation. God told Noah that the rainbow would be a sign of His everlasting promise that He would never again flood the whole earth or wipe out creation. God said when He sets the rainbow in the sky, He would look upon it and remember His promise to mankind. You could have knocked me over with a feather.

I thought, "Oh! That's why everyone loves rainbows and

stops to look at one whenever it shows up in the sky! The rainbow is a promise from God! Wow. He even gave us something visible and beautiful to see in our world to remind us that He cares for us and keeps His promises to us!"

Later, as I pondered this tangible sign of a promise from God, I thought about the fact that God said *He* would look upon the rainbow and remember His promise to us. Awestruck, I thought, "*God* is also looking at the rainbow when we're looking at the rainbow? No wonder humans will practically wreck a car to get a glimpse at a rainbow in the sky! It's like a two-way mirror into heaven!"

If I couldn't knock *you* over with a feather right now, then let's break it down a bit more. How evil do you think God considers mankind in this day and age? Better or worse than Noah's time? If God was sorry He made mankind, and was so disgusted at their lives that He destroyed everyone but eight people and a few animals, what do you think God would like to do to us now given the evil in our world at this time? Don't you think He'd like to crush it and try to forget how many times mankind broke His heart? Why doesn't He?

Because He said that He wouldn't destroy creation that way again. Because He said so. There really can be no other explanation if you believe that God exists. If you believe that God is good, then what's the reason we're still stumbling through this life?

The answer lies in your Bible. First, because He said that He wouldn't destroy all creation again, He won't. Second, and you'll find this in your Bible as well, God won't end this life on earth until all the things that He said were going to happen come true. I'm quite certain there are other reasons known to the Creator and not to us, but there are enough in the Bible to convince me that God knows the appointed time and it hasn't happened yet. But it will. Because He said so and God always keeps His promises.

As you encounter "the stretch" in your own grief journey, may I encourage you to say something like this to yourself (sometimes I even write it over and over):

> this life is a vapor
> this life is so short compared to eternity
> I get all of eternity with my kids
> this life is a mere breath, a passing shadow
> I can do this
> God promised to fix this
> God promised heaven and eternity
> God will fix this

You could also memorize or keep Psalm 39:4–5 in a place where you can see it every day:

> O Lord, make me know my end
>   and what is the measure of my days;
>   let me know how fleeting I am!
> Behold, you have made my days a few handbreadths,
>   and my lifetime is as nothing before you.
> Surely all mankind stands as a mere breath!

God keeps His promises, my friend. Heaven and eternity are waiting for you. Do you know what God said about heaven? Here's a small slice for you:

*Then I saw a new heaven and a new earth,
for the first heaven and the first earth had passed away,
and the sea was no more. And I saw the holy city, new
Jerusalem, coming down out of heaven from God,
prepared as a bride adorned for her husband.*

*And I heard a loud voice from the throne saying,
"Behold, the dwelling place of God is with man.
He will dwell with them, and they will be his people,
and God himself will be with them as their God.
He will wipe away every tear from their eyes, and death
shall be no more, neither shall there be mourning,
nor crying, nor pain anymore,
for the former things have passed away."*

*And he who was seated on the throne said, "Behold, I am
making all things new." Also he said, "Write this down,
for these words are trustworthy and true."
And he said to me, "It is done! I am the Alpha and the
Omega, the beginning and the end. To the thirsty I will
give from the spring of the water of life without payment.
The one who conquers will have this heritage,
and I will be his God and he will be my son."*
(REVELATION 21:1–7)

God has promised that He will wipe every tear from our eyes. God has promised that we will have no more death, no more mourning, no more crying, and no more pain. When the stretch of this life feels like more than you can handle, remember that God always does what He says He's going to do. Someday, you will mourn no more!

God has promised that Jesus would offer the spring of the water of life without payment (you don't have to earn heaven), and the one who conquers her disbelief and puts her faith in Jesus will have heaven as her inheritance. She will be His daughter. It is done!

Keeping your eyes on eternity is how you conquer the stretch of life without your child. You are waiting for heaven, which will be only wonderful forever and ever . . . and ever . . . and ever.

SURVIVAL STEP:
Remember That Life Is Truly Short

If you think about the time, whether it's years or days, that you had with your child, you cannot help but see how time flies. Look at old photographs of yourself, or watch a TV show from your youth. The truth is that this life is short. It may feel insurmountably long right now, but that is grief talking, not truth. Years go by quickly. Time keeps passing at a faster and faster rate as we get older. Try to keep your mind focused on heaven, eternity. Keep reminding yourself that your life is like a passing shadow, brief and always moving. When grief tries to trick you into thinking that you simply cannot live the rest of your life without your child, remember that God said He would fix this world, someday, somehow. He *will* do it. This pain is only a breath. You can do it.

Ideas:

- Develop a mantra of sorts. Tell yourself the truth: this life is short. Write it down.
- Put up pictures of yourself as a teenager, when you thought you had all the time in the world.
- Put up pictures of your lost child as a newborn, and remember that time goes by so quickly.
- Write Psalm 39:4–5 and Revelation 21:1–7, and keep them tucked somewhere in your car or purse.
- Print a picture of a beautiful rainbow to remind you that God keeps His promises.
- Listen to the song "There Will Be a Day" by Jeremy Camp or "One Day" by Matt Redman.
- Get up before sunrise and watch how fast the sun makes the morning light into a new day.
- Try to think about what you did last month. Can't remember much? Likely not. Time goes by too quickly!
- Take time to enjoy nature. A beautiful walk always reminds me that there are seasons that keep turning and yet seem to roll quickly from one to the other.

SPIRITUAL STEP:
Write Ten Promises from God

Even if you are not sure you believe any of this about God or Jesus, you could Google "promises of God," and several results will show up for you to read and think about. If you are a brand-new believer in Jesus, do the same thing, but you should also ask your pastor or someone at church to walk you through this exercise in the Bible. If you have been a Christian for a while, you can probably think of ten, but I would encourage you to locate them in your Bible and write them down from Scripture.

In addition to writing ten promises from God, develop some practical ideas for how you can remember that this life is short compared to the eternal glory we will inherit as Christ-followers.

Ideas:

- Mark Psalms 39:4–5 and 144:4 ("man at his best is a mere breath"; "his days are like a passing shadow"; NASB) in your Bible, and post them in places in your home or office.
- Read Revelation 21 and 22 about the new heaven and earth.
- Read Isaiah 64–66 about the new heaven and earth.

- Read Genesis 7–9 about Noah and the ark and God's promise to creation.
- Keep the ten promises of God somewhere you can read them every day. To help get you started, here are a few of the promises that I cling to:
  - God loves me. I am precious and honored in His sight. (Isa. 43:4)
  - God "is near to the brokenhearted and saves the crushed in spirit." (Ps. 34:18)
  - God has prepared a place for me in heaven. (John 14:1–7)
  - Jesus promised the Holy Spirit will be my Helper forever. (John 14:16–17)
  - Through Jesus, God forgives all my sin, and this forgiveness is available for everyone. (John 14:1–7; Acts 2:36–39; Heb. 8:12)
  - Someday, God will wipe every tear from my eyes and will create a new heaven and a new earth where there will be no more death, mourning, pain, or crying. (Rev. 21:1–7)
  - In the meantime, God has promised to be with me always. He will never leave me or forsake me. (Matt. 28:16–20)

while you wait for heaven: finding purpose in the here and now

What now?

Now that you've faced your worst fear, walked through the stench of death and grief. Now that you've faced the stretch of the rest of your life in front of you without your child. Now what do you do? Life after losing a child can feel like it's "on hold," and all you are really doing is waiting to go to heaven so your family can be complete again. Waiting for heaven is tough. You need something to help you focus, to help you make the wait worthwhile. Otherwise, the stretch will swallow you up, and grief will win. Giving your pain an outlet, using your grief for something good, can make the time pass faster and give you purpose for the here and now.

> *Blessed be the God and Father of our Lord Jesus Christ,*
> *the Father of mercies and God of all comfort,*
> *who comforts us in all our affliction, so that we may be*
> *able to comfort those who are in any affliction,*
> *with the comfort with which we ourselves are comforted*
> *by God. For as we share abundantly in Christ's*
> *sufferings, so through Christ we share abundantly*
> *in comfort too.*
> (2 CORINTHIANS 1:3–5)

In the verse above, it says that we are comforted by God so that we can, in turn, comfort others with the comfort we received from God. Oh, how I hope and pray you have been comforted by God during your reading of this book, through your grief journey. I pray you have felt His mighty presence, power, and comfort in some tangible ways.

You'll need it. You'll need God for this next step, perhaps as much as you needed Him to drag you out of the pit of grieving a child. Now, my fellow sojourner of the valley of the shadow of death, you offer your pain back to God as a love offering. You ask God to use your pain and suffering to comfort someone in need. I must warn you that it will not be easy. I have been fighting against writing this book for years. The cost is so high.

In order to use your pain to comfort others, you'll have to face it again. You will have to remember what it felt like in the early days. Each stage of healing must be remembered. Reflection and soul searching will be required. Most of all, you'll beg God to make sure you don't have to stay back in that pit for very long. "I'll go back, God, to help this person, but pull me back out quick!" were my thoughts each day as I wrote for you. As I cried, stomped, curled up in a ball, yelled, and sobbed my way back through all these memories, I leaned into my God. I asked Him to give me a feeling of certainty that the pain would not be as intense, as long-standing, or as deep as the last time I fought my way out of the pit.

Did God answer my cry for help? Yes, He did. I felt His hand and beautiful love with every keystroke. Remember that one thing I've learned with certainty on this grief journey: God does what He says He's going to do. God said He would never leave us or forsake us (see Heb. 13:5; Deut. 31:6–8; Josh. 1:5). Our God would not ask me to walk alone back through the pain of losing Austin. He promised to never leave me or forsake me. Since we're told to comfort others with the same comfort we have received from Him, God knows what He is asking of us. It only stands to reason that God will equip us to go forward and comfort others.

> In order to use your pain to comfort others, you'll have to face it again.

You may have heard the saying "your mess is your message." I believe this is a true statement, and it seems to fit with the verse above about comforting others. That being said, however, I needed to be a bit further out of my "mess" before I was able to transform it into any sort of "message."

If you are still early in your grief journey, then relax and soak up the comfort from others and God. You'll have time to help. Just like on an airplane when they tell you to put on your own oxygen mask before you help someone else, you must heal before you can comfort others. Take your time. Work on your relationship with God. Make strong those relationships in your family. Stay connected to friends. When the time is right, you'll feel the nudge to begin offering your pain to help someone else.

The ways that you could help someone else are endless. The idea is to do something, *anything*, to help others in some way. I noticed that when I was able to shift my focus off my grief, the heartache faded to the background for a while. As you begin to help others, you will get some relief from the pain. Early on, your effort to help others does not have to be related to losing a child or grieving. Any simple act of kindness pointed at someone else has the power to soothe your soul.

At some point, you need to lift your chin and step back into the world. Taking that step because someone else needs your help seems to make it a bit easier. I believe it is the outward focus on loving another person that enables a grieving parent to reenter the presence of others without falling apart. The power of love and kindness are just as strong when poured out (maybe more so) as they are when received. No one but you can know when you are ready to minister to someone else, but let me encourage you to make it sooner rather than later.

A good indicator of your readiness might be whether you are able to get through your ordinary days, for the most part, without curling up into a ball on the bathroom floor. Keep in mind that you will have rough days, some really rough days, for a very long time. Don't let those days stop you from helping someone else on one of your good days. Within the first couple of years, you don't really know when a good day or a bad day is going to happen. So, if you are in your first few years of walking on this planet without your child, I would keep your efforts to help others very flexible. Try something that you can "book" or "cancel" on any given day.

If you are further along in your effort to stay out of the pit of grief, then you might be ready to take on a role, task, or program to help others that is more demanding. Perhaps you are ready to take some responsibility or position that needs your input and attention at certain times or set days. Either way, beginning to think about other hurting people is a powerful healing tool that I recommend. Start small and work your way into more demanding ideas. Let thoughts of someone else and someone else's struggle occupy your heart. Give grief a kick to the curb for a few moments a week and see how it feels.

I need to add one cautionary note. When you are thinking of doing something to help another person, consider whether you could keep a happy heart if that person began to complain about his/her struggle. My empathy for others was so very low for such a long time. If anyone around me began to express a difficulty, my mind would shout at them: "Really?! You are going to complain about that when my child is dead?

Seriously?" I had to be careful about extending a helpful hand when, in my heart, I wanted to use that hand to smack them instead. You can't really love on a person when your insides want to scream. The other person won't feel the love of God through you if your internal self is struggling to smile.

The fix for me was to choose people to help whom I considered to have it "worse" than me (by my standard in my head). Coming alongside someone who I thought was dealt a heavier blow than me also helped me to see that I was, in fact, still grateful for many things in my life. Helping others helped restore my empathy—over time—A LOT of time. Now that I am much farther along in this journey, I am able to see other hurts and circumstances and feel how a person could have serious struggles in life, even if all her children are alive.

There are still days and circumstances, however, when I am having a tough day, that I know my ability to have compassion or empathy for others is low. On those days, I try to keep to myself, if I can. For the most part, shifting my focus toward others remains a source of healing for me. Helping someone else makes my "on hold" time pass by more quickly. I know it can do the same for you.

SURVIVAL STEP:
Help Someone

When you are able to get through many of your ordinary days, start making a list of people who need help. Think of the types of people who you would think might "have it as bad as you." The list may be small, but I'm sure you could think of a couple of types of people who are suffering as much as, if not more than, you are. For example, moms who have sons in prison touched my heart.

I cannot imagine visiting my son in prison for the rest of his life, as some of the women I've met in a prayer support group have had to do. Those sweet ladies told me they make it through the prison visits because they always tell themselves, "At least I'm not visiting a grave." For me, I'm glad I'm not visiting Austin in prison. I'm relieved that his life was full of fun and then he went straight to heaven. I also cannot imagine being the parent of a missing child, or a murdered child.

Gratitude also fills my heart because Austin had three healthy, vibrant years with us. Helping parents whose child has lived (or did live) a life of sickness with surgeries, hospital visits, chemo, and so on is a way of expressing compassion for parents who have not known the gift of a healthy child.

The short list of people who have been dealt a similar or worse set of circumstances is where I recommend you start serving, just one time a month, when you are having a good day. Start simple and work your way into something more substantial as your heart heals. The list below contains only a few examples of ways other parents have spent their time on this planet while they are waiting on heaven. I pray that it kick-starts you into something beautiful, and that it helps turn your mourning into dancing as you love others.

Ideas:

- Pass out blankets and doughnuts to the homeless.
- Knit baby blankets for mothers who deliver a stillborn or critically ill baby.
- Make care packages for the moms of inmates.
- Create unique jewelry pieces for mothers who've miscarried babies.
- Join a prayer group for parents of missing children.
- Find a way to serve families with kids in cancer treatment.
- Send cards or thank-you notes to military personnel deployed outside the US.
- Help collect prom dresses for girls who cannot afford them.
- Collect gently used baseball equipment, and deliver it to a community that might need it.
- Serve in an organization fighting against human trafficking.
- Volunteer at an animal shelter.
- Deliver a meal to an elderly neighbor.

SPIRITUAL STEP:
Pray for Others

All the recipients of the helpful ideas above could use prayer as well. The missionaries working in dangerous places need prayer. Our police officers and firefighters, our congressmen and women, and our president also need to be covered in prayer. The list of people you could pray for is endless.

Be intentional about spending a few minutes each day praying for someone else. I find that starting my day by shifting my prayers away from my own grief seems to set the tone for my day. When I make a point to pray for others in the morning, those days seem to go forward in a more positive way, with an outward focus. Reminding myself that others are hurting and struggling helps me get out of my own head. It may sound strange, but thinking and praying about someone else's nightmare instead of your own is a great way to start your day.

Use the list you created above to make a list of people or groups of people you could pray for in earnest and from your broken heart. Train your mind to shift away from your grief and onto others. Discipline your soul to be grateful for the blessings that remain in your life by praying for the hardships of others.

You'll find that praying for others, like everything else, is easier on some days and more difficult on other days. There are days when it is a struggle to pray for others because my mind is swimming in memories or trapped by the replay of that horrific morning. On those difficult days, I try to tap into my stubborn and hardheaded self. I try to dig up some determination and force myself to pray for at least three people before I give up.

Usually, I'll dive into my Bible next. If I can't seem to pray, then I replace that prayer time with some Bible time or

playing worship songs that wash over me. If you stop praying and don't fill the time with something else that is focused
on God, the morning is likely to begin with self focus. On
the journey of grief, a self-centered start to the day is a sure
trap into a bad day. Dwelling in your grief is sure to follow
a prayer session that was cut short. When that happens, the
enemy wins again. Refuse to let that happen. Cry out to God
for help, force yourself to pray for someone else at least for a
few minutes, and then shift gears into worship music, Bible
time, or service to others. You have to fight deep darkness
with prayer. It works!

Ideas:

- Get a prayer journal and write down your prayers.
- Make a list of names or groups you want to pray for each
  week.
- Ask others to join you in praying for a certain group of
  people.
- Send one card a week to someone you know who needs
  your prayers.
- Start a Facebook group dedicated to praying for a cer-
  tain person or group.
- Use Twitter to post a prayer for someone else each day
  (keeping confidentiality when needed, of course).
- Set an alarm or an appointment on your phone two
  times per day to remind you to pray for others.
- Use the beginning of your lunch hour to pray for others.

- Get a book of prayer devotionals.
- Make a playlist of three songs, and commit to praying for others while you listen to those songs.
- Draw or color while you pray for others.
- As you read your Bible, change the verses into a prayer for someone. Just hours before His death, Jesus prayed for His disciples and future believers. Go to that prayer and pray those words over others (John 17:20–26).
- Use a prayer app (there are several good ones!) to help you organize and remember to pray for others.

steppin' forward

We will close out our journey as we began it—with truth. You will never be the same. The one year grieving period most experts assign to the death of a loved one is simply not adequate for the loss of a child. I have read some books or articles that suggest the loss of a child takes "more like two years." I very much disagree with the two-year grieving period as well.

You will never stop grieving your child. As long as we breathe air and exist on this planet, we will grieve our child. I cried every single day that I wrote this book, and Austin died ten years ago. I'll never be "over it." I am, however, in a much better place than I was even five years ago.

Try not to place expectations for "better" on your life.

Each year does seem to generally ease some of the pain and sadness. I wouldn't say that the pain has gone away but rather that I've gotten better at managing my grief. As a result, my life might look like I'm "better" after ten years. As only parents who've lost children can know, however, "better" is a relative term and very precarious. "Better" can be lost in a moment, in a memory. Down I go again into the deep, dark pit of grief.

I've accepted that the pit of grief will remain in my life for the rest of my days. What I won't accept is that I have to *live* in there. I don't. I won't. With God, I can climb out of that pit every single time I fall back in there. You can too.

Don't put a time limit on your grief. Try not to place expectations for "better" on your life. Take it one day at a time, one step at a time, one moment at a time. Little by little, like those waves crashing over the seashells, your grief will get smoother, smaller, and lighter.

SURVIVAL STEP AND SPIRITUAL STEP:
Commit to climbing out of the pit of grief each day, one day at a time, and ask God to help you through each moment.

We have a saying for this final step in the grieving process in the Erickson house (in fact, my husband got it tattooed on his back!): Steppin' Forward.

We use this motto of sorts to remind us that we must make a choice, every single day, to grab God's hand and step forward, out of the pit of grief, and into each new day. We say it as a toast, we say it some mornings as a greeting, and we say it during tough days as we flop exhausted into bed.

It seems only appropriate that I pass this motto on to you,

my new friend. Picture me raising my coffee cup, looking right into your tear-filled eyes, and lifting my chin in stubborn determination: Here's to Steppin' Forward . . . Every. Single. Day.

closing thoughts

It's bittersweet to be writing these final words to you. I am torn between gladness and emptiness. Gladness because I no longer, for this book, have to trudge through the darkest parts of living without Austin. Emptiness because I'll be letting go of your hand and will no longer have your consistent companionship to lighten this load called grief. My hope is that I've lightened your load a bit, too. The purpose of this season is ending for me, but I hope our connection will remain.

As grief continues to circle and surprise you, I pray you'll pick up this book and remember that you are not alone. My deepest desire is that you would turn to God first and seek His face for the comfort only He can provide. My best advice is to turn to the Gospel of John and search the heart of Jesus for your healing.

As you approach chapter 13, I encourage you to read the next five chapters (John 13–17) with your last moment with your child in mind. John 13–17 is *that* moment for the disciples of Jesus. Just after the meal, teaching, and prayer described in these chapters, Jesus was arrested and killed. You know how you can recall every little detail about those final minutes with your child? John 13–17 describe *those* minutes for Jesus and the disciples. Years later, I'm sure the disciples could remember where they sat around the table, what they ate, what the room smelled like, etc. Making these moments even more powerful, Jesus *knew* these were His last words to them before His death, and I believe He knew the disciples would cling to these words (just like we do) after He was gone. And just like we cling to last moments and last words with our dear ones, so the disciples cherished those last hours in the upper room.

The Gospel of John, and specifically chapters 13–17, changed my life and helped me keep living in those first few years after Austin died and even today, because I can tell how much God loves me when I read those chapters. Studying these chapters for several years led me to write a Bible study called *His Last Words: What Jesus Taught and Prayed in His Final Hours.* The desire for *His Last Words* is to help other women understand the love of God and Jesus. I invite you to study the last words of Jesus so that your heart may heal and you can rest in confidence that God is good and always keeps His promises.

I want to leave you with this picture of my family.

Does it hurt a bit because Austin's smiling face is not in the picture with us? Yes. It still hurts even a decade later. But, please notice that we are *together*. We are *smiling*. We are *happy*. When you think that you can bear no more, I want you to flip here, to the end of this book, and see that the Erickson family made it to a time when we have more happy moments than sad. If we made it, you and your family can, too. Turn to God, cling to each other, and cherish the blessings you still have in your life. Step forward, one day at a time, and don't give up. May the Lord shine His light upon You during these darkest days, and may you allow God to help you, hour by hour.

Closing Prayer:

Father God, please make Your presence known to this mother. When she crumples to the ground in her grief, will You allow her to feel Your arms around her? Talk to her, Lord. Let her hear Your voice. She's so lonely and tired, Lord. Lift her up, dry her tears, and stop that searing pain in her heart. Guard her heart *and* her mind, Father God. Stop any attacks from the enemy before they ever reach her or her family and friends. Put a hedge of protection around them, Lord. Help her with anxiety and worry; stop those things from destroying what she has left in this life. Lord, only You could restore peace and joy to this family. Only You. I plead with You to do it now and do it quickly, Father God. You can help this mom step forward. Let her feel You and see You so that she can learn to live again, one moment at a time, relying on You to help her get through this unimaginable loss. You are a great and mighty God who can do anything. Do this for her: let her feel Your love now more than ever before. Let Your love overwhelm her. Let Your joy and peace fill her. In Your power, and by the name of Jesus, I pray. Amen.

resources

Websites and Groups:

GriefShare: https://www.griefshare.org/

Compassionate Friends: https://www.compassionatefriends
.org/

While We're Waiting Facebook Group: https://www.facebook
.com/whilewearewaiting/

National Helpline for Addiction and Suicide Prevention:
https://www.samhsa.gov/find-help/national-helpline

Cancer.Net: https://www.cancer.net/coping-with-cancer/
managing-emotions/grief-and-loss/grieving-loss-child

Books:

*Grieving the Loss of a Loved One: A Devotional of Comfort as
You Mourn* by Kathe Wunnenberg

Streams in the Desert devotional book by L. B. Cowman

Heaven by Randy Alcorn

Heaven for Kids by Randy Alcorn

Safe in the Arms of God by John MacArthur

Choosing to See by Mary Beth Chapman

acknowledgments

I would not have been able to bear the loss of Austin or had the ability to write this book without God. My relationship with Jesus and almighty God through the work of the Holy Spirit makes all things possible, including surviving sorrow such as this. So, thanks be to God. Blessed be the name of the Lord who gives and takes away. Yet, blessed be His name.

Without a husband who not only believes in me but supports me in so many tangible ways, this book would not have been written. Thank you, Devin, for all that you are and all that you continue to be to me and our family. You amaze me and inspire me every single day. Ethan, please know how much joy you bring to our lives. You are the strength and inspiration for so many things in our family. I pray that one day you'll be able to see yourself through the eyes of our Lord and embrace all that He has planned for you and your life.

To my parents, for showing me that life does, indeed, go on after losing a child, and for teaching me that living joyfully is a choice. To my sister, Pam, who always cares for me and cheers me on, even on the hardest days. I'm so blessed to call you sister and friend. To my brother, Mike, who is the solid rock in our family. Thank you for standing so steady in your faith and love.

Next, thank you to Erica Wiggenhorn and my Bible Study Crew (Amber, Beth, Emily, Katie, Mawiyah, Melvina, and Rachel). Without the encouragement and downright badgering from some of these women, I would have remained in stubborn disobedience to the Lord's call to write this book. Thank you for being true friends and standing in the gap for me when I couldn't do it for myself. Thank you for being brave enough to push me to finally write and finish this book. Your unwavering support and prayers appear on every page and in every sentence. There are no words for the gift of such friendship. Thank you, Lord, for these women.

Thank you, Judy Dunagan, for being such an inspiration to me. Your sweet spirit and love for the Lord shine so brightly that I can't help but be guided closer to God. I'll be forever grateful that the Lord decided we could create books together for Moody Publishers. I'm in humble awe to be part of such a privilege. Thank you for your Spirit-led guidance and encouragement. May the Lord continue to bless your family and the work of your hands and heart.

Thank you, Betsey Newenhuyse, for your dedication to this book in spite of your own pain of just losing your beloved husband, Fritz. Your willingness to help others through a deep grieving process while you are steeped in your own is an inspiration to me and a wonder to others. What a beautiful example of this verse you are:

Blessed be the God and Father of our Lord Jesus Christ,
the Father of mercies and God of all comfort,
who comforts us in all our affliction, so that we may
be able to comfort those who are in any affliction,
with the comfort with which we ourselves
are comforted by God.
(2 COR. 1:3–4)

Finally, thanks to the Moody Publishers team, who work so hard to support and equip the church. Your work reaches broken hearts every single day. I pray that you always feel the Lord blessing you and your work. Thanks for all that you do for the kingdom of God.

about the author

Kim Erickson began following Christ after the death of her three-year-old son from strep throat in 2008. Her growing relationship with the Lord and the Bible saved her from the pit of grieving the loss of a child. She developed a deep, abiding love for the Word of God and began a writing and speaking ministry. Her website is www.KimAErickson.com.

Kim's writing and speaking ministry is dedicated to equipping others with an understanding of the promises God made to us. Her heart is to inspire people who are struggling to focus on eternal perspectives. Kim challenges you to live each day filled with the outrageous joy and peace that comes from a deep relationship with God.

Kim is the author of *His Last Words*, a Bible study of the Gospel of John, chapters 13–17 (Moody, 2017).

She has appeared on the *Building Relationships* radio program with Dr. Gary Chapman (*5 Love Languages*), *Chris Fabry Live!*, and several other Moody Radio programs. Chris Fabry described Kim's story as "one of the most powerful stories I've heard." In addition, Kim has participated in podcasts designed to encourage women to draw closer to God. The radio interviews and podcasts can be found on Kim's website.

Kim also is an attorney who practiced business litigation for thirteen years before becoming a law professor. She lives in Florida with her husband, Devin, and son, Ethan.

Imagine knowing you only have several more hours to live

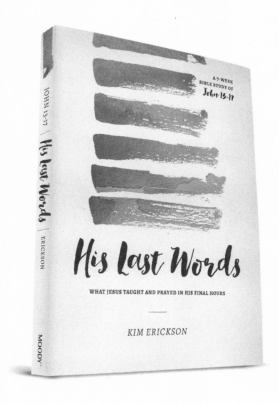

The 5 Love Languages® for Grieving Parents

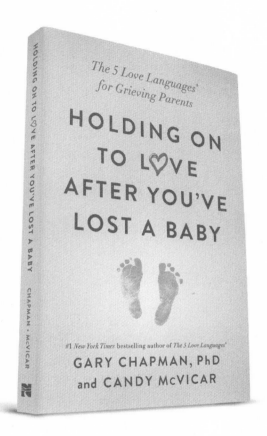

There is no pain like the pain of losing a child. For anyone facing this loss, *Holding onto Love After You've Lost a Baby* is for you. With relationship expert Gary Chapman and Candy McVicar, you'll learn how the five love languages can help you grieve well and pursue healing.

978-0-8024-1940-8